Can We Talk?

To Dianne,
whose love and devotion are teaching me
what communication is really all about

Luke 6:38

Can We Talk?

Sharing Your Faith
in a Pre-Christian World

Robert G. Tuttle, Jr.

Abingdon Press

Nashville

CAN WE TALK?
SHARING YOUR FAITH IN A PRE-CHRISTIAN WORLD

Copyright © 1999 by Abingdon Press

All rights reserved.

This book is printed on acid-free paper.

Library of Congress Cataloging-in-Publication Data

Tuttle, Robert G., 1941-
    Can we talk? : sharing your faith in a pre-Christian world / Robert G. Tuttle.
    p.   cm.
Includes bibliographical references.
ISBN 0-687-08416-4 (alk. paper)
1. Evangelistic work—Philosophy.   2. Christianity and culture.   I. Title.
BV3793.T88 1999
266—dc21

99-39691
CIP

99 00 01 02 03 04 05 06 07 08—10 9 8 7 6 5 4 3 2 1

MANUFACTURED IN THE UNITED STATES OF AMERICA

Contents

Introduction 9

Chapter One: The Rationale 17

Chapter Two: The Biblical Mandate 27

Chapter Three: The Search Begins 35

Chapter Four: Transcultural Common Denominators

(or Dynamic Equivalents) 41

Chapter Five: The Key 53

Chapter Six: A Transcultural Gospel 61

Chapter Seven: The Principles Applied: The Case Studies 75

Chapter Eight: Putting It All to Work—for You 93

Conclusion 107

Introduction

It was obvious that I was getting nowhere in a conversation at a dinner party with a new acquaintance who had made an honest inquiry regarding my faith in Jesus Christ. I blushed as I finally asked somewhat tentatively, "Are we communicating?"

The response I received was not totally unexpected, "I'm terribly sorry, but I don't have a clue what you are talking about." Admittedly, this person was unchurched, with little exposure to Christianity, but this was not a hostile environment. The man was open and friendly. I was in my own town among some of my closest friends. I simply was not communicating. Much of the terminology that had been effective for years was no longer working. Theology that seems to be irrelevant is, in fact, irrelevant. Then, after several similar experiences, I decided it was time to do some serious retooling. This book is a result of that attempt.

For several years now I've been most concerned with communicating the gospel of Jesus Christ in cross-cultural settings. I have traveled the world looking for a gospel that was transcultural in its appeal. Imagine my surprise when I realized that "cross-cultural" is no longer just across some international border. It is across the street, even across the dinner table, sometimes in my own home. Almost ten years ago a news magazine announced that in the twenty-first century, racial and ethnic groups will outnumber whites in America for the first time.[1] Furthermore, immigrant groups bring with them their native languages and customs. Their children attend the public schools and add cultural richness, but they also challenge the school systems with their educational needs. In one elementary school in New York City, the children represent families where any one of twenty-six different languages, from Armenian to Urdu, is spoken at home. On our good days, we live in a society that is diverse in that it is pluralistic, multiethnic, and multicultural. On our bad days, we live in a society that is not only secular but perverse and openly pagan. Most communicators are now willing to affirm that fact, but few, as yet, are ready to face its implications.

The so-called postmodern world is more than a fad phrase. It describes a mind-set (even in the West) oblivious to many of the more traditional approaches bent on logic and reason in the presentation of the gospel. George Hunter in *Church for the Unchurched* (Nashville: Abingdon Press, 1996) writes that "modernity has not fulfilled most of its promises, and so the Enlightenment worldview has become increasingly vulnerable" (p. 22). Modernity (dated roughly from the fall of the Bastille in 1789 to the disintegration of the Soviet Union two centuries later) did not produce a rational basis for consensus morality. In fact, there seems to be little or no consensus in any field of endeavor. There is even a "high" and "low" postmodernity. Communication in terms of low postmodernity relates to life on the streets. It attempts to describe how things are, but has a difficult time articulating this. Discussions of high postmodernity are relatively articulate but have few (if any) certainties. For many of my postmodern friends, convictions are out: convictions are okay for me, but don't let my convictions impinge on them. They rejoice in differences. No single source has all the answers. There is no reality, no absolute, until they own it. Some umpires call 'em the way they see 'em. Some call 'em the way they are. Postmodern thought is adamant: they ain't nothin' till I call 'em. Postmodern thinkers are so obsessed with the past (for example, the musical *Grease* is a '90s remake of a '70s musical recollection of a '50s musical phenomenon) that they have a difficult time

1. "Remapping American Culture," *U.S. News & World Report*, Dec. 4, 1989; p. 28.

grasping the future. It can become superficial to them. I'm reminded of a Tokyo Santa Claus nailed to a cross. Postmodernism wants to sample everything. It is ten miles wide and half an inch deep. Remember Robinson Crusoe's goat fence? The fenced-in area was so wide that the goats on the inside of the fence were just as wild as the goats on the outside of the fence.

In an increasingly secular world, there seems to be no firm place to stand in order to begin an appeal. The significant cultural changes that used to take thirty to forty years now take less than five. Most students now entering college have never seen a black and white TV. To them, the host of *The Tonight Show* has always been Jay Leno. Change is all around us. Yet, for all its challenges, postmodernism still gives spirituality a place at the table. Suddenly I realized that the research I had amassed for other cultures was just as relevant for my own. I began to ask some serious questions.

A TRANSCULTURAL GOSPEL?

Is there a transcultural gospel—**an introduction to the gospel that communicates with more or less equal effectiveness across cultural boundaries, both at home and abroad?** Is there some form of the good news that we can share with the world at large that is a step beyond "pre-evangelism" but that is prerequisite to the more detailed presentations to follow? Are there things that we can assume about the people we encounter (regardless of their presuppositions) in Chicago, in Bangkok, in New York, in Tel Aviv, in Peoria, in Lagos, in Seattle, or in Moscow, that would access an increased receptivity to the gospel? Are there common denominators that are truly transcultural (common to every culture) and genuinely relevant? Even postmodernity is relative only in some areas. What about education (2 plus 2 still equals 4)? What about highway and street signs (red lights still mean stop)?

So, for me, the search for such a gospel has been the work of a lifetime. I am forever foraging for tools to make the gospel of Jesus Christ more user-friendly in cross-cultural settings. The more "classic"

(Western) approaches to the presentation of the good news of Jesus Christ seem to beg the issue, especially outside—but more increasingly inside—our own culture. For example, the "Evangelism Explosion" question, "If you were to die tonight, do you know for certain that you would go to heaven?" might be effective, if one's view of heaven is positive enough to motivate a response; but there are other questions behind that question (even more basic to a common core) that transcend cultural boundaries. If we are to find a transcultural gospel, we must address the issues that touch people where they live, perhaps somewhat less (perhaps somewhat more) sophisticated than the Campus Crusade for Christ "Four Spiritual Laws."

TRANSCULTURAL "FOUR SPIRITUAL LAWS"?

I am not certain that I like the sound of this question, but is there a transcultural equivalent to the Campus Crusade for Christ Four Spiritual Laws (paraphrased below)?

- God loves you and has a wonderful plan for your life.
- All have sinned and are, therefore, alienated from God.
- Jesus Christ is God's only provision for sin. Through him you can know and experience God's love and plan for your life.
- Therefore, put your faith and trust in him.

Although this approach seems to be too one-dimensional (simplistic), too culturally bound (Western), and too linear (straight line), well-meaning "missionaries" have used these "laws" more or less effectively on university campuses for years.

While attending seminary, I dropped in on a Campus Crusade meeting in a fraternity house on the campus of Northwestern University. Although the time spent was well invested, I shall never forget the reaction of one of the students, "How come no matter what the question is, you always give the same answer?" My knee-jerk response was "Jesus is the answer to every question," but somehow I knew that I had done neither him nor Jesus justice.

12

THE QUESTION

A transcultural gospel refuses to give the answer before it hears the question. The "question," that's the point! So, first, what questions are people asking around the world that can best be answered by a winsome and intelligent presentation of the gospel of Jesus Christ? Then, what would that multidimensional, winsome, and intelligent presentation look like in a cross-cultural setting?

Some years ago I began teaching a course entitled "Cross-cultural Evangelism." Right from the start I used several case studies to illustrate the importance of being sensitive to cultural issues. I listened carefully to a missionary named Don Richardson share such a case—"The Peace Child."[2] This particular case sparked an interest.

After several years of failure in his missionary endeavors, Richardson was in despair. He had suggested that two warring Sawi tribes in New Guinea move their villages closer together, thinking that proximity would foster reconciliation. Retribution, acted out through betrayal and deceit, was the Sawi sign of power and prestige. In the story of the Crucifixion, for example, Judas, not Jesus, held their attention. So the village move simply made it easier for them to kill one another. Finally, Richardson summoned the two chiefs and informed them of his intent to leave—he had failed. Surprisingly, the two chiefs, not wanting to lose a missionary whose considerable investment (not to mention his medical knowledge) had saved many lives, made the following vow: "Tomorrow we will make peace."

The next day the tribes assembled. Richardson watched curiously. What could possibly affect peace, overnight, when he had labored for years with little result? At dawn the tribes came together and the two chiefs exchanged infant children from their own families. The tradition, unknown to Richardson, was to exchange sons with the understanding that as long as the children lived, no retribution could be enacted between tribes. Peace was instantaneous.

When Richardson asked, "Why?" the response was, "It is our culture." Richardson then asked, "Could you have exchanged the sons

2. See *Christian Theology*, edited by Robert Evans and Thomas Parker (New York: Harper & Row, 1976), pp. 108-12.

from another family?" The immediate reply was, "Of course not. It must be our own sons." Richardson's response was obvious, "There is an interesting precedent for that . . . " (now Judas was no longer the champion, but the villain who betrayed the peace child), and the gospel was finally communicated through a powerful redemptive analogy.

Richardson insists that such analogies can be found in every culture. Children, for example, are cross-cultural, even **transcultural** (a term preferred to cross-cultural, since **trans**cultural implies commonality not simply from one particular culture to another, but throughout every culture). I remember the historical breakthrough at Camp David between Jimmy Carter and Anwar Sadat when the two began to talk about their grandchildren. Around the world children laugh, cry, and even ridicule each other (nyah, nyah, nyah, nyah, nyah) in the same language. So, what about other transcultural common denominators? I decided to do some hands-on research. Since it is important to experience peoples in their own environments if we are to test the effectiveness of our communication, once again I set off around the world searching for clues for a transcultural gospel among the people I encountered. Throughout Asia, the Middle East, Africa, Europe, and Latin America, I looked for concepts, and even ideologies, that communicate with more or less equal effectiveness across cultural boundaries. Then, after returning home, I continued my research in some of the urban and rural areas of North America. Hundreds of interviews conducted during that time of research and travel provided most of the insights that I want to share with you here. Let me illustrate with some additional dialogue from the dinner party encounter with my new acquaintance mentioned at the outset of the introduction.

"YOU'VE GOT TO HAVE A HOIST"

After adjusting to the awkwardness of my initial inability to communicate, I decided to ask a straightforward question, "Have you ever considered Christianity?"

14

He smiled, "No, why should I?"

He seemed genuinely interested so I asked, "What do you do for a living?"

"I am an engineer," he replied.

For some reason, I then asked, "What do you do when you've got a fifty-ton block of concrete? How do you move it?"

His immediate response, "You've got to have a hoist."

My next comment, "Let me tell you about the hoist," opened the door for some interesting conversation. Over the next few minutes I began in a very introductory way to share with him my own conviction that every religion the world over (including my own) was like a fifty-ton block of concrete without the enabling power of the Holy Spirit available through personal faith in Jesus Christ. Even though he had not yet heard of the Holy Spirit, did not understand faith, and knew "Jesus Christ" as little more than a swear word, I attempted to explain briefly that to place one's faith and trust in Jesus Christ as Savior and Lord is to experience the promise of God who gives us the Holy Spirit—the hoist—who empowers us to live life victoriously, even abundantly.[3] As we left for the evening I lifted my arm like a hoist—"Don't forget the hoist." The next week at the home of a friend he noticed me across a crowded room, smiled, and lifted his hand, mimicking a hoist. Ah, a beginning—as you will soon see, we have had several interesting conversations since. Once again, that encounter sent me scurrying to find other clues relevant for a presentation of the gospel that is truly transcultural, both at home and abroad. Let's take a look.

---

3. I found it interesting that among most pre-Christians not only is Jesus Christ a swear word, but the Holy Spirit implies something like cosmic fluff; personal means none of your business; and faith tries to believe in something not quite receivable.

CHAPTER ONE

The Rationale

Perhaps it would be good to begin our inquiry by setting the record straight with two significant disclaimers.

THE FIRST DISCLAIMER

I have often said that the presentation of the gospel can be described in two words—hard work. The search for a transcultural gospel is not for the benefit of some generic shortcut that preempts the consideration of even tougher questions to follow. I will emphasize again and again that the principles discussed here simply provide tools for that "first step"—the initial cross-cultural encounter. The more detailed work of discipleship (usually within community) must then lead to the more careful analysis of peoples in culture. To communicate at one level does not mean that the work of evangelism has been done.

Closely related to this idea is the principle that no single approach to the gospel will communicate to everyone, especially in cross-cultural settings. I recently read a dissertation on the use of Japanese haiku poetry as a tool for gaining insight into the Asian culture and was struck by a twelfth-century definition of "good man." Let me paraphrase it: A good man is one who is so immersed in history, literature, poetry, and religious doctrine that he is sensitive to the feelings of others, responsive to nature in all of its manifestations, and acutely conscious of the vulnerability of beauty, the brevity of worldly things, and the pathos of the human condition. Contrast that with the understanding of "good man" in some other cultures: macho, heroic, mechanical, intellectual, self-sufficient, entrepreneurial—alas, the task is before us.

Again, **the intent here is not to find some magical formula, but to suggest tools** for use as initial points of contact to take us beyond the realm of "pre-evangelism." Is there access to that first step within "universal" experience?

An awareness of this "first step" was John Wesley's peculiar genius. He knew the mind of his eighteenth-century audience. In a manner typical of the eighteenth-century evangelical revival, Wesley would walk the early morning streets of a small English town with an entourage of twenty to thirty Methodists. As they marched toward the market cross—usually located in the town center, frequently within sight of a dismal gallows—they would sing hymns to attract a crowd. Wesley would then preach for ten or fifteen minutes (no longer), beginning with the lowest common denominator—usually on the topic of death or hell—just to get their attention. The invitation at the end of these sermons was not so much to accept Christ as to "fear God and flee the wrath to come." At that point the entourage would circulate among those responding to the invitation, signing them up—on the spot—for a class meeting that afternoon. Wesley would then rely on the class meetings to make the more in-depth appeal. Is it surprising that the majority of converts in the Wesleyan Revival were won to Jesus Christ one-on-one, in class meetings?

Is John Wesley's eighteenth-century approach transcultural? Probably not. My friend at the dinner party would not have been impressed. Death, for him—as I found out later—was no threat. As in many cultures, death had an appeal, the promise of a better life, perhaps in some reincarnated form. Shintoism and some of the Islamic cults glorify death (especially the "noble" suicide) as the door to eternal bliss. Many of the Egyptian pharaohs spent more money on their tombs than on their palaces. Death was simply the flour of the loaf baked by the gods. In many so-called Third World countries death may be feared by individuals but is so visible (contrary to the West where our corpses are disguised to look like department-store mannequins) that it barely turns the head. Once, on the way to an airport in China I noticed that the bicycles ahead of us were avoiding something in the middle of the road. Since I thought it was a dead animal, you can imagine my shock to see the body of a woman, left to rot in the sun. I've seen similar things in several other countries as well.

So, here is the question: Since death and hell are not much of a threat to the universal mind, are there transcultural common denominators that can attract the world's attention?

THE SECOND DISCLAIMER

A second disclaimer is that the term "transcultural gospel" should not imply universalism. I do not for a moment believe that all religions are the same. Admittedly, most attempts at finding a transcultural gospel look for the answers in other religions—what Buddhism, Hinduism, and Islam already share in common with Christianity. Although there is some truth to that approach, for me that is the wrong point of departure since all religions (again, recalling my friend at the dinner party) are fifty-ton blocks of concrete if they lack the power to measure up.

So, let's be honest. I believe that Christianity presses on where every other religion leaves off. That, however, does not make me right and the rest of the world wrong. Over the years students have asked, "How can you be so narrow-minded as to assume the uniqueness of faith in Jesus Christ?" My response, "My believing in the uniqueness of faith in Jesus Christ doesn't make me right, but it sure makes me an evangelist."

I do not mean to sound glib, but I'm not into Christianity for the pain. I'm into Christianity because it is the only way I know how to survive. If you know someone or something that accesses the power of God better than faith and trust in Jesus Christ, then please let me in on your secret. You have my undivided attention. I know full well that if God is a triangle and I believe that God is a circle, God does not become a circle to accommodate what I believe God to be. God remains a triangle. Truth has never changed to accommodate what I believe truth to be. Nevertheless, I believe that it is faith in Jesus Christ alone that puts us right with God, heals the brokenness of our time, and makes us fit to share the heritage of God's glory. Jesus states clearly, on the eve of the Crucifixion, within the shadow of the cross, "I am the way and the truth and the life. No one comes to the Father except through me" (John 14:6). If you can convince me otherwise—that Jesus is not who he said he was and is—I am a dead man. Flesh would not cling to bone any longer. You could gather me up in a basket. That's just how much of me is at stake.

CHRISTIANITY AS WORLD-AFFIRMING

I also believe that Christianity is, or should be, different in its basic approach to life and creation. There is much in the world of religion that is world-denying. It tends to imply dualism—a good God and an evil god. The good God dwells within us, while the evil god (perhaps some Neoplatonic demiurge) creates the universe and the world in which we live.[1] Since creation is evil, salvation calls us out of the world ("let the world go hang") by contemplating the God within, that we might be united to (or perhaps absorbed by) some kind of Cosmic Fluff.

Christianity, on the other hand, at its best is world-affirming. Although some forms of Christianity insist that happiness in this world is only an illusion, I believe that the same God whose Spirit dwells within us is the One God who creates; and in spite of the fact that creation has fallen, God wants it back for our enjoyment. Creation is far more important to God than to the devil. Similarly, God is not some kind of cosmic killjoy. I sometimes tell my students that if

---

1. "Demiurge" (within the Neoplatonic or Gnostic system) denotes a supernatural being that was imagined as creating the world in subordination to the God of the Bible (at best), or that was (at worst) sometime referred to as the originator of evil.

20

they can't have more fun doing God's thing than the world can doing it own thing, then they should give their faith another look. Something is missing.

In less than six months after I began teaching at the E. Stanley Jones School of World Mission and Evangelism on the campus of Asbury Theological Seminary, several of my colleagues helped me see that Christians have conceded far too much to worldwide anti-Christian influences. For example, the evangelistic emphasis on the so-called "10/40 Window" (those European, African, and Asian countries that lie between the 10th and 40th parallels) assumes Satan's control of great masses of people and gives little or no thought to the prevenient work of the Holy Spirit already in place.[2] Modernism (especially among Christians) was obsessed with the influence of the demonic, no doubt looking for some reasonable explanation for the problem of evil (theodicy). Postmodernism seems far more open to the work of the Spirit. Although I would be the first to admit that the "10/40" attempt to establish a prayer base upon which to begin evangelistic ministries is noble, I am reminded again and again that God has more invested in creation than we do. God is already at work, and if we can find the tools to communicate the gospel effectively, then God might well let us in on the fun of winning this world to Christ. Permit me one more illustration from John Wesley.

Soon after his Aldersgate experience, Wesley preached a sermon entitled "The Almost Christian."[3] In that sermon he spoke about the faith of the "almost Christian" and the faith of the "altogether Christian." There, the faith of the almost Christian implied a "heathen honesty" that paid at least some regard to truth and justice that was expressed in love and offered in assistance to one another. It also implied a "form of godliness" that abstained from excess and honestly sought to avoid all strife and contention. The almost Christian frequently prayed and was sincere toward inward principles of religion, extending even to a real design to do the will of God. Unfor-

2. "Prevenient grace" is the Holy Spirit at work in everyone between conception and conversion. The Holy Spirit woos or prevents us from moving toward extreme disobedience, so that when we finally understand the claim of the gospel upon our lives, we are guaranteed the freedom to say yes.
3. *The Works of John Wesley*, ed. Albert Outler (Nashville: Abingdon Press, 1984), 1:131-41.

tunately, according to the earlier Wesley, since the almost Christian lacked the one necessary thing evident in the altogether Christian—the faith that follows repentance and offers the forgiveness of sins—all of this, though noble when enlivened by believing in the Son who brings everlasting life, served only to compound the almost Christian's condemnation.

Half a century later Wesley wrote a sermon entitled "On Faith."[4] In this sermon he contrasted the faith of a servant with the faith of a child. Here the faith of the servant is directly analogous to the faith of the almost Christian referred to in his earlier sermon. Now, however, the faith of the servant, rather than serving only to compound the servant's condemnation, means that the servant is not far from the kingdom of God.

Like the "10/40 Window," the "Almost Christian" sermon concedes too much to the enemy (the "Accuser"), whereas the later sermon, "On Faith," acknowledges the influence of the Holy Spirit already at work in the world. Once John Wesley recognized that evangelism is bearing witness to a God already at work, a God who walks the streets of every city and hamlet the world over, ministry became less of a chore and more of an opportunity. His *Works* demonstrate that perspective time and again. Wesley became more and more sensitive to cross-cultural issues that would further the appeal of the gospel, and enrich the effects of the eighteenth-century evangelical revival.

THE UNIVERSAL WORK OF THE HOLY SPIRIT

I assume that the Holy Spirit is at work in everyone, everywhere. This conviction, linked with the need to be culturally sensitive in order to cooperate with the work of the Spirit, is the rationale for this book. As strange as this may sound, if God loves some people more than others, I'm not sure I want to go to heaven. If God is no respecter of persons, then admittedly the Holy Spirit must somehow take up

4. Ibid., 3:492-501.

the slack and level the playing field. Forgive my presumption, but since I believe that faith in Jesus Christ is the only way, then **God, by the prevenient work of the Holy Spirit, must guarantee that every man, woman, and child has an equal opportunity to respond, if not to the name, at least to the person of Jesus Christ.** How can that be? How can one respond to the person of Jesus Christ without knowing his name?

It occurs to me that knowing someone is far more than knowing his or her name. Early in his ministry Wesley condemned some of the mystics because they did not specifically call people to faith in Jesus Christ. These mystics were the "rock on which [he nearly] made shipwreck."[5] Of all the enemies of revival they were the worst because they stabbed Christianity in the vitals, making a mockery of personal faith in Jesus Christ. Later in his ministry, however, Wesley used examples of several of these mystical lives to illustrate Christian perfection. Obviously, one cannot have it both ways. So, what happened to change his mind? As he matured in his theology, Wesley began to rely more and more on the fruit of the Spirit (Gal. 5:22) as the criterion for faith. His conclusion? Even if it looked like a grapevine, if it produced apples, call it an apple tree. So, if the mystical lives manifested fruit that only faith could produce, then faith must be present, even without the mystics acknowledging it.

Jesus says, "Not everyone who says to me, 'Lord, Lord,' will enter the kingdom of heaven, but only he [or she] who does the will of my Father who is in heaven" (Matt. 7:21). Obviously I can know someone's person without knowing his or her name. I have gone to remote parts of the world and among those open to the Holy Spirit already at work within them, spoken the name of Jesus, and received this response: "So that's his name." Jesus says to his disciples, "Everyone who listens to the Father and learns from him comes to me" (John 6:45). Furthermore, "The Holy Spirit, whom the Father will send in my name, will teach you all things. The Spirit of truth who goes out from the Father, he will testify about me; he will convict the world of guilt in regard to sin and righteousness and judgment; he will guide you into all truth" (John 14:26; 15:26; 16:8, 13). I am absolutely con-

5. The Works of John Wesley, ed. Frank Baker (Oxford: Oxford University Press, 1980), 25:487.

vinced that in those who remain open to the Spirit, a personal relationship with God will lead inevitably to faith in the person of Jesus Christ, and if his name is spoken, a recognition of that name will confirm their experience. Let me illustrate.

I have a close friend named Betty who tells of an experience in China. Seeing an opportunity for ministry, she and her husband had gone there to teach English as a second language. Although their primary task was to teach English, as Christians they found plenty of opportunities to share their faith in Jesus Christ. Over the course of several weeks Betty had gotten fairly well acquainted with several of her students. One of these students (we will call her Hannah, since to use her Chinese name would place her in jeopardy) seemed open and teachable yet especially resistant to the gospel. Although the Temple of Heaven in Beijing might have given her at least some reference to God and the eternal, she would laugh and become argumentative with any reference to the name of Jesus. Between themselves, Betty and her husband began referring to her as "Hard-hearted Hannah." Then, however, Hannah's true spirit began to surface.

It was Betty's custom to rise early and go to the dining room to pray. On one such occasion she realized that Hannah (who was preparing the tables for breakfast) had been watching. Somewhat to Betty's surprise, Hannah approached her and asked respectfully, "Betty, what are you doing?" Immediately, in spite of Hannah's former resistance, Betty realized that the Holy Spirit was at work. Without apology she said, "I'm praying." Hannah asked, "What's 'praying' mean?" Betty added, "It is talking to my heavenly Father in Jesus' name." This time Hannah did not resist but asked further, "What does that mean, talking to your heavenly Father in Jesus' name?" Betty then explained, "It's just telling him what I need, asking for forgiveness, and asking for his guidance in everything that I do. He cares about my everyday activities, even my aches and pains. I pray in Jesus' name because faith in him assures the forgiveness of my sins and that seems to make my prayers more personal and give them more power. Jesus says in our Bible that 'anyone who has seen me has seen the Father . . . and that I am in the Father, and that the Father is in me' " (John 14:9, 10). No doubt this Bible quotation, along with "He cares about our everyday activities," got Hannah's attention. She then asked if Betty would pray to God, in Jesus' name, to protect her two brothers who were learning to drive a truck, a dangerous occupation in that part of China. Betty promised she would.

The next day, after breakfast, Betty had an impulse. She said to Hannah, "Hannah, I'm in real pain. My back is hurting. Would you pray to God to make my back better?" Hannah said, "I still do not know what prayer is." Once again, Betty explained that praying to God is just like talking to your best friend. Imagine Betty's delight when Hannah bowed her head and prayed, "Hello, God, this is Hannah speaking. You don't know me. I don't even know how to say these words, but please make Betty's back feel better. Please help our American teachers as they help our Chinese teachers to speak English. Help the Chinese teachers with their pronunciation so they can speak and understand the English words. In Jesus' name I pray this prayer. Amen." Smiling, Hannah then asked if that was the correct way to pray. Betty assured her that it was.

The next day, since Betty's back was better and her own brothers were safe, Hannah, quite unsolicited, asked if she could pray again. This time she prayed, "Hello, God, this is Hannah again. Do you remember me? I'm Betty's friend. I spoke to you yesterday about Betty's back. Now I want to talk about her daughter who is having a baby. By the way, are you only a 'western God,' do I have to talk to you in English? Do you understand Chinese? In Jesus' name. Amen." Betty smiled and gave her a hug.

In a few short weeks, simply by remaining open to the Spirit at work within her and talking to God as she would to a friend, Hannah not only learned how to pray (in Chinese as well as in English), but came to know the person of Jesus Christ and acknowledged his name without further resistance. Hannah and Betty still correspond.

I have no doubt that this encounter was the work of God, leading Hannah "to the Father, through the Son, by the Holy Spirit."

Let me give you another illustration closer to home. Remember my friend at the dinner party? As we became better acquainted, it was apparent to me that he genuinely cared about people. As a husband and father, he was loving and considerate. I watched him closely as he related to his wife and children. As an engineer, he was vitally interested in issues concerning the safety of others, even at the expense of criticism (and some ridicule) from colleagues and friends. I was impressed, perhaps a bit envious. I became convinced that the Spirit was at work, that this man was not far from the kingdom of God. Who knows, one day I might speak the name of Jesus in answer to a relevant question only to hear him reply, "So that's his name."

Again, put this universal work of the Spirit together with a sensitivity to culture in order to communicate the gospel, and the rationale for this book is complete. Now, let's build this rationale upon biblical grounds.

CHAPTER TWO

The Biblical Mandate

Although I believe that the Bible alone (at least from a theological point of view) contains the only universal truth, it is clear to me that a search for the presentation of a transcultural gospel should begin not in religion (including my own), but in people and culture. What is there in people and culture that can be used as a transferable concept (a dynamic equivalent) for communicating the good news of Jesus Christ? The Old and New Testaments set a pretty good precedent.

THE OLD TESTAMENT

If God had told the author of the Pentateuch just how this old world was put together, he (or she) never would have written anything down. I am forever admonishing my students to think Hebrew, not Greek. In Genesis, the Greek mind wanted to know exactly how it happened (talk about modernism). The Hebrew mind simply wanted to know who did it (postmodernism has a precedent as well). In Revelation, the Greek wanted to know whether or not the streets of heaven were paved with gold. The Hebrew wanted to know whether or not Jesus was coming back. The Greek was always caught up in the detail (who got to the tomb first). The Hebrew wanted the bigger picture (whether or not Jesus rose). You would think that quantum physics would have taught us something with its images of the particle and the wave. The particle is obsessed with the detail. The wave is embraced by the greater truth.

God in the Creation account (Genesis 1–11) does not run roughshod over culture. Scholars tell us that there were contemporary myths that were similar in some respects to the biblical account of creation. Some see this as a threat to the integrity of the Old Testament. Let me give this a different twist. God wanted to communicate the truth of a divine purpose and (it is suggested) used some of the existing stories from Mesopotamia as transferable concepts to reveal a universal truth. People in the days of Moses knew and supposedly understood these stories. God does not have to start from scratch. The bits and pieces of reality in the existing myths are cleaned up, sanctified, and woven into a narrative that people could understand. Although the difference between Creation as the result of the one God, loving (the Genesis account), and many gods, warring (the Mesopotamia account), is significant, the overall story is communicated in such a way that people could relate and understand. **The existing culture is used as a springboard for communicating divine revelation.** Is God smart or what? This is one of the principles we need to explore in our search for a transcultural gospel. Another principle, however, takes this same concept to still another level.

Within generations of Adam and Eve, God regretted having created our first forebears. It is a bit of an understatement to be reminded that the flood seriously pruned the family tree. Unfortunately, it is a short journey from Noah to Babel. Humankind, still sin-prone, once again yielded to inherent desire. God knew that humankind, in community, left to itself, would have perfected its own evil and destroyed itself. There is nothing we cannot do when community is of one mind—in consensus. *Unredeemed,* we would have perfected our self-centeredness and devoured ourselves. Perhaps God separated us at Babel to prevent our self-destruction. The confusion of languages served to preserve a remnant that could understand the reality of only *one* God. It has recently occurred to me that Babel, the last paragraph of primeval (undated) history, mandates the study of different cultures (Gen. 11:8-9). We need not return to Babel, but we must find ways of communicating across cultural boundaries. In fact, the first paragraph of patriarchal history, the covenant established between God and Abraham (Gen. 11:10-17), demonstrates the principle of using a culture to communicate divine revelation. In effect, the last of primeval history sets the stage for cross-cultural studies.

The story of Abraham is another example where God (and the author of the Pentateuch) uses existing culture to communicate the truth. I've had students complain that the covenant with Abraham makes God appear too bloodthirsty. My response is usually "God didn't invent the concept of covenant. That was already in place when God chose to be revealed."

How did you establish relationship in Abraham's day? You "cut a covenant." God's use of the covenant is God's way of being culturally sensitive. God related to Abraham in a way that Abraham could understand. According to custom, the animal was sacrificed and the two parties of the covenant, Abraham and God (symbolized by the fire pot), passed between the halves of the divided animal with the promise that if either broke the covenant, the same fate would befall them. There were even provisions for covenant renewal. Feast days were established where animal sacrifices—as signs of repentance—underscored the seriousness of sin. After several generations, however, these acts of sacrifice degenerated into a form of religion that no longer demonstrated the heart. God wearied, once again, but had promised never again to destroy or confuse creation. In God's infinite mercy a new covenant was established where God provided a complete and perfect sacrifice that would take away the sins of the world, *once and for all*. Nestled in the middle of the longest book in the Bible we find these words:

> "The time is coming," declares the LORD, "when I will make a new covenant with the house of Israel and with the house of Judah. It will not be like the covenant I made with their forefathers when I took them by the hand to lead them out of Egypt, because they broke my covenant, though I was a husband to them," declares the LORD.
>
> "No longer will a man teach his neighbor, or a man his brother, say-

ing, 'Know the LORD,' because they will all know me, from the least of them to the greatest.... For I will forgive their wickedness and will remember their sins no more." (Jer. 31:31-32, 34)

First Peter 1:17-21 states that "the precious blood of Christ, a lamb without blemish or defect ... was chosen *before the creation* of the world" (emphasis added). The implication here is clear. God took the cultural concept of covenant seriously. From the beginning God knew full well that the very act of Creation itself would eventually require the blood of an only Son. It is terribly significant that **God was a Redeemer before God was a Creator. God loved before God made.** Even though the covenant with God was broken time and again, God established a guarantee that our brokenness would no longer rule and that our sins would be remembered no more.

Indulge a brief aside to illustrate this point. There is a wonderful story that originates during the latter part of the Middle Ages about a young girl who had visions of Jesus. The Inquisition, intolerant of such experiences, sought to intimidate her and would summon her before their tribunals. On one such occasion the Chief Inquisitor challenged her while sneering, "The next time you see Jesus ask him what sins I confessed at my last confessional." The following week she was summoned once again. Laughing, the Inquisitor asked, "Well, did you see Jesus?"

Remarkably unafraid, she replied simply, "Yes."

Suddenly the entire assembly was attentive as the Inquisitor continued, "And what sins did I confess?"

The little girl smiled, "Jesus said, 'Tell him, I forgot.'"

Listening to a friend tell that story recently I suddenly got an image. As I watched that scene in my mind, I realized that the little girl was surrounded by a host of angels (see Matt. 18:10), and much to my surprise, these were no ordinary angels. These angels were huge, hairy, and mean-looking. Some had tattoos. Some wore tennis shoes. Then, as I looked even closer, I realized that every angel was carrying a large millstone. Not surprisingly, each millstone was etched with the text of Luke 17:2 ("It would be better for him to be thrown into the sea with a millstone tied around his neck than for him to cause one of these little ones to sin").

Does God's initiative in establishing a covenant sacrifice that would guarantee victory over sin and death make God bloodthirsty? I think not! Remember, God did not invent the rites of covenant. Covenant relationship (recalling Richardson's "redemptive analogy" demonstrated with his story of the "Peace Child") is God's attempt to be culturally sensitive to a concept already in place so that love and forgiveness are communicated in a way that could be understood and received. God is always taking such initiative, in all times and in all places.

THE NEW TESTAMENT

The New Testament sheds even more light on this issue. The biblical mandate to motivate believers to communicate the gospel the world over is not just in the Great Commission—"Go and make disciples of all nations"—but in the Great Commandment—"Love the Lord your God . . . and your neighbor as yourself." Again, God was a Lover before God was a Maker. I do not love in order to evangelize. I evangelize because I love. There is a world of difference. One smacks of manipulation, the other of compassion. Predictably the Bible itself provides the best illustration.

Acts 16 describes the beginning of Paul's second missionary journey. It is significant that Paul has now been called to Macedonia after the Spirit of God had prevented Paul and his companions from entering the province of Asia and then Bithynia. Apparently, God not only opens doors but shuts doors as well (if I really believed that, I should probably rejoice just as much with the one as with the other—hmmm).

Macedonia was virtually a land without Jews. Even though only ten married Jews were required to establish a synagogue, there was no synagogue in Philippi, "a Roman colony and the leading city of [the] district" (16:12). So, on the Sabbath, Paul walked outside the city gate to a river where he expected to find a place of prayer. For a Jew, this must have seemed like the end of the world. Yet when Paul encountered Lydia, "a dealer in purple cloth from the city of

Thyatira," the Spirit of God had already "opened her heart to respond to Paul's message" (16:14). God had already taken the initiative in the drama of rescue. Prevenient grace (the influence of the Holy Spirit that goes before) was already at work. Although the conversation that Paul had with Lydia is not recorded, you can well believe that a message that was truly transcultural was the catalyst for her conversion.

Now look at the next chapter of Acts. Paul is at Athens, attempting to communicate the gospel to a culture that believed in many gods. They even had an altar to an "Unknown God"—just in case. Paul makes his appeal, and here the actual content of his message is given. Pointing to the altar of this unknown god, Paul states:

> Now what you worship as something unknown I am going to proclaim to you.
>
> "The God who made the world and everything in it is the Lord of heaven and earth and does not live in temples built by hands. And he is not served by human hands, as if he needed anything, because he himself gives all men life and breath and everything else. From one man he made every nation of men, that they should inhabit the whole earth; and he determined the times set for them and the exact places where they should live. God did this so that men would seek him and perhaps reach out for him and find him, though he is not far from each one of us. 'For in him we live and move and have our being.' ...
>
> "Therefore since we are God's offspring, we should not think that the divine being is like gold or silver or stone—an image made by man's design and skill. In the past God overlooked such ignorance, but now he commands all people everywhere to repent. For he has set a day when he will judge the world with justice by the man he has appointed. He has given proof of this to all men by raising him from the dead." (Acts 17:23-28, 29-31)

Is this transcultural? Paul used what was at hand to communicate the gospel of Jesus Christ. God (who "is not far from each one of us") was already there preparing the hearts of men and women who "became followers of Paul and believed" (17:34).

There are other similar stories that are even more dramatic. In Acts 10 we find Peter going to Cornelius. Peter, a purist Jew, goes to a centurion in Caesarea to preach to a family that had already been visited by God. The same Spirit that had been poured out on the Jews at Pentecost was now poured out on this Gentile family in a Gentile city.

It is significant that the mystery referred to by Paul in Ephesians is not that Gentiles would be converted (that was predicted in the Old Testament), but that Jews and Gentiles should be included in the *same* body.

Consider the story of the eunuch in Acts 8. Once again the Holy Spirit takes the initiative. In this instance Philip is told by an angel of the Lord to go south along the road to Gaza. There he meets the eunuch from Ethiopia who is reading the book of Isaiah. Judge for yourself whether or not the Spirit of God was already at work preparing the eunuch to receive Philip's message.

> "Do you understand what you are reading?" Philip asked [the eunuch].
> "How can I," he said, "unless someone explains it to me?" So he invited Philip to come up and sit with him.
> The eunuch was reading this passage of Scripture:
> "He was led like a sheep to the slaughter . . ." [See Isa. 53:7.]
> The eunuch asked Philip, "Tell me, please, who is the prophet talking about, himself or someone else?" Then Philip began with that very passage of Scripture and told him the good news about Jesus. (Acts 8:30-32, 34-35)

Isaiah was not only talking about Jesus, but a few chapters later he would be talking about the eunuch as well. As they continued reading in the book of Isaiah, they found these words:

> Let no foreigner who has bound himself to the LORD say, "The LORD will surely exclude me from his people." And let not any *eunuch* complain, "I am only a dry tree."
> For this is what the LORD says: "To the *eunuchs* who keep my Sabbaths, who choose what pleases me and hold fast to my covenant—to them I will give within my temple and its walls a memorial and a name better than sons and daughters; I will give them an everlasting name that will not be cut off." (Isa. 56:3-5, emphasis added)

Little wonder the eunuch was then baptized by Philip and went on his way rejoicing.

In my book *Sanctity Without Starch*, I tell a story about an encounter on an airplane. I shared the gospel with a businessman during the flight. After the plane landed, the businessman and I both walked into the airport lobby. Someone was waiting there to whisk me off to a preaching appointment. Much to my surprise, the businessman took my ride by the lapels and said an interesting thing: "I've just had the most incredible experience of my life and I promised God that I would witness to the first person I saw when I left the plane and you're it. I was about to make a decision that was better for profit than for people and with God as my witness, I have determined to be an oppressor of people no more!"

Imagine my surprise when the businessman then pointed his finger at me and said: "I'm this man's eunuch." While it was occurring to me that if my ride did not know the Bible, I could be in trouble, my friend explained. As with the Ethiopian eunuch, God had prepared his heart to receive the message of the gospel.

By way of summary, let me restate the general thrust of this chapter. Although I believe that absolute truth (again, from a theological point of view) can be found in Scripture alone (all subsequent truth must be measured in light of that truth and must never contradict it), the search for a transcultural gospel must begin in people and culture. People such as my friend at the dinner party have convinced me that just because I have the truth there is no guarantee that the world will listen. I must find transferable concepts that will communicate that truth. Culture supplies the key. The Bible sets the precedent. The question now is, Are there keys that will guide us, not only within culture but across cultural boundaries, to a transcultural gospel? What questions are most relevant for the universal "man," whether an American engineer or a common laborer in the rice fields of inland China? What are the issues unique to the gospel, yet relevant to those whose hearts have been wooed, but not yet fully convinced, by the work of the Spirit? The search begins.

CHAPTER THREE

The Search Begins

As I have already mentioned, over the past twenty years I have been traveling with a specific agenda. Although other activities, such as sermons and lectures, often consumed my time, I was always looking for clues from my experiences with new acquaintances that would enable me to communicate the gospel in cross-cultural settings. On airplanes, trains, buses, and even taxis, in public places or private homes, I would conduct interviews, seeking a fairly good sampling from all the different cultures.

THE INTERVIEWS

Frequently, just to break the ice, I would ask my new acquaintance if he or she would like to see a portfolio of photographs (nearly one hundred in all). Although urban and rural settings got different recognition (and most of these images are somewhat culturally specific), the following were nearly always recognizable by a significant cross-section of every culture:

Men playing soccer
The Taj Mahal

The White House
Abba (rock group)
Women playing basketball
The Beatles
Elvis Presley
Madonna
The Dome of the Rock
U2 (a rock group)
A Buddha
Marlboro cigarettes
Big Ben
Ayatollah Khomeini
Gandhi
A Buddhist monk
A crucifix
A water buffalo
A chessboard
A cobra
Mao Tse-tung
A giraffe
A cross
The Bible
The Koran
Michael Jordan
Pelé
An elephant
Coca-Cola
A Ping-Pong match
McDonald's
Muhammad Ali
The Great Pyramid

Admittedly, simple recognition might not tell us a great deal. My sister tells me of an experience she had while teaching in China. A young man took two bamboo sticks and fashioned a beautiful cross as a gift. Then, after his gift was gratefully accepted, he asked, "What does cross mean?"

Furthermore, what about the images that were not universally recognizable? They may teach us something as well. Here are a few examples:

> The Kremlin
> Mickey Mouse
> Mother Teresa
> The Eiffel Tower
> A minaret
> A picture of Jesus
> Maps
> The Great Wall of China
> The Mona Lisa
> A football
> A church steeple
> A Hindu temple

Let me give you another instrument for interviews in looking for transcultural common denominators. Most of the time I asked questions that were (I hoped) *not* culturally specific:

- What is the most important thing in your life?
- What do you think about before you go to sleep?
- What do you dream about?
- What do you think about first thing in the morning?
- Is there one thing that supplies the ruling force for your life?
- What activities consume most of your time?
- What frightens you?
- What interests you?
- What excites you?
- What gives you joy or pleasure?

For some, the answers to these questions were easy. For others, they were not so easy. Little wonder I am becoming more and more of an anthropologist and, as a result, a better and better theologian.

It might surprise you to learn what I have found. Let's put some of this together. Perhaps it is best to begin with the obvious.

CHILDREN

No surprises here. We have already learned with the story of the "Peace Child" that children are of universal concern. On a train ride from Yanji (Manchuria) to Beijing I sat across from a couple taking their son to a hospital to be treated for cancer. Since I could speak no Mandarin it was difficult to communicate, yet it was obvious that the boy was ill. After ten hours I was getting nowhere with my attempts to relate. At one point, I simply pointed skyward (alas, a pre-Copernican universe where heaven is up), folded my hands as if to pray, and then pointed to the boy. The communication was instantaneous. Immediately, several others were summoned to interpret. Smiles, handshakes, and even gifts were exchanged throughout the cabin. We talked for hours. I learned that this trip to the hospital was taking all of their life savings. Although they were "officially" atheists, concern for a child had opened a door to a conversation about God.

If the care of children often elicits sacrifice, then the abuse of children arouses outrage. Some years ago a man confessed to me at a communion rail during a worship service that he had molested his daughter, his granddaughter, and was now molesting his great-granddaughter. I still remember the anger that I felt. What I said to him surprised even me. With full conviction I said that one of two things was going to take place that very night. Either he was going to get the serious kind of help that would prevent him from ever molesting another child, or he was going to jail. Most people do not know just how difficult it is to believe that God loves us if we were abused as children. Little wonder that in an Asian culture children must not be approached by a stranger unless the parent of the child initiates the contact.

In an airport in Bombay, India, I had an opportunity to become acquainted with a Muslim while we were both waiting for a delayed flight. We decided to share a meal. I soon learned that he had been born in Kenya, was teaching at the University of London, and spent several months a year in India researching the growth of crops for food. Within minutes the conversation somehow turned to God. He confessed that his wife had recently had a religious experience and was teaching their seven-year-old daughter how to pray. Somewhat to his dismay the child had been pleading with him to pray with her as well, but he simply could not bring himself to do it. I said to myself, "You jerk, why don't you pray with your daughter?" Then I asked out loud, "You believe in God, why won't you pray with your daughter?" He replied, "Yes, I believe in God, but why would God want to hear my prayers?" In a flash (and so help me, I have no idea where this came from if not from God) I responded, "I'm going to tell you a story."

"On your return home your plane lands in London. You work your way through passport control and customs and as you exit the security area you are hard to miss, (he must have weighed over 400 pounds), so she sees you before you see her. Suddenly you hear, 'Daddy, Daddy,' as she works her way through the crowd. Then, as she struggles free from the mass of people she runs across the open space and jumps into your arms, hugging and kissing you, saying all the while, 'Daddy, Daddy, you are the most wonderful daddy in the whole wide world.' How would that make you feel?" As I looked at him I could see tears beginning to form. He replied, "You know how that would make me feel. It would make me feel wonderful." I simply added, "So, why would God be any different?" He concluded with a smile, "I can't wait to get home and pray with my daughter." The care and concern for children is transcultural.

Now, before moving on to another chapter, permit me one more brief aside (which anticipates important concepts soon to follow). God's gift of a son can be universally understood—absolute genius. God was first revealed in the flesh not as a father or mother, not even as an adult, but as a child. With growing anticipation that child became more and more aware of just who he was. As that child became a man, the realization of his mission became clear and he shared that mission with others. Eventually this mission led to a cross—a sacrifice eternal in the heavens—and then culminated with the Resurrection—that we too might live eternally. It should be no surprise that the Child himself speaks directly to the point: "I tell you the truth, unless you change and become like little children, you will never enter the kingdom of heaven" (Matt. 18:3). Then again: "Let the little children come to me, and do not hinder them, for the kingdom of heaven belongs to such as these" (Matt. 19:14).

I've already mentioned that my friend at the dinner party was a devoted father. Not too long ago I asked him, "You're a pacifist. Someone could threaten your life, but what about the lives of your children?" I could tell by looking at him what his answer would be, "Mess with me, but don't mess with my kids." I knew I was on to something. We were really starting to communicate, at least at one level.

So, the search for a transcultural gospel had begun, but this was just the beginning. It is time to press this concept even further.

CHAPTER FOUR

Transcultural Common Denominators (or Dynamic Equivalents)

In the introduction I stated that throughout my research I was looking for transcultural common denominators (sometimes referred to by anthropologists as "dynamic equivalents"), concepts and even ideologies that communicate with more or less equal effectiveness within as well as across cultural boundaries. This should not imply that there are not other needs (food, clothing, shelter, safety) more basic to our survival. Certainly those needs are vital. The church must and should address those needs constantly and habitually. Here, however, we look for other areas of common interest that can open doors for communication in the fields of evangelism. We have just seen that the love and care for children is transcultural. There are other common denominators that can assist us in a search for a transcultural gospel. Some should be obvious, but others might surprise you.

COMPETITIVE SPORTS

Typical of the American male is that he turns first to the sports section of the local newspaper. I teach near Lexington, Kentucky, where basketball rules supreme (even above horse racing, although most of the thoroughbreds sold around the world are raised on the more than four hundred horse farms throughout the area). A few years ago, Rick Pitino, then coach of the University of Kentucky men's basketball team, resigned to take a position in Boston with a professional team. The next day every page of the entire first section of the *Lexington Herald-Leader* only had articles related to his leaving. Even the weather map showed the weather in Boston.

It is said that every available space in Japan is covered with rice paddies, tea fields, or baseball diamonds. Latin America and Europe are consumed with soccer. I was amazed that in most Asian countries basketball is the craze. We were in parts of China where small villages seemingly had but one electric light and that was over a basketball hoop; and the enthusiasts played most of the night. At one point I had a student with me who could slam dunk a basketball. All he had to do was demonstrate and the people would flock—instant communication.

Just the way one approaches a sport can provide a transferable concept. If a stronger player demonstrates courtesy and sportsmanship, then the others frequently respond in kind. Conversation between games can easily turn to the subject of Jesus without giving offense. If we had just had the stamina, evangelistic opportunities were available to us all night long on basketball courts all over that part of the world.

In Israel I was staying at a hostel at the foot of Masada. In A.D. 70 the people of Masada had committed suicide rather than surrender to impending slavery by the Roman captors who had built ramparts against their mountain walls. In the hostel there were seventy-five to a hundred people sharing large dormitory-type rooms and common tables for eating. For several hours I attempted to engage some of the other guests in conversation, but no one seemed interested. During the evening meal I found it difficult to communicate, even with those who sat directly across the table. I felt invisible.

After dinner a young Frenchman was challenging all comers to a game of chess. He was apparently the current champion of the hostel and so intimidated the group that no one dared to take him on. Then, seeing me, he offered me the challenge. Since I've played a bit of chess, and I do love an adventure, I accepted. Immediately fifty to sixty people gathered round, cheering for the underdog—me. As the game developed, the Frenchman became overconfident and careless. I defeated him in twenty moves—instant communication. Suddenly I was a celebrity. They asked me to speak. Somewhat embarrassed I asked, "About what?" Their reply, "Tell us your story." In situations such as this, I usually try for simplicity. I told them how my visit to Masada had enriched my experience of a living God, a God who loved us and cared for us and could deliver us from slavery of any sort. They listened.

The next day, I decided to climb to the top of Masada by foot rather than take the cable car. On the trail I was approached by a young man who had heard me speak the night before and was curious to know more. At the top of the mountain I told him about the power of the Holy Spirit available through faith in Jesus Christ. He was open and receptive. We corresponded for years.

The psalmist writes:

> In the heavens he has pitched a tent for the sun,
> which is like a bridegroom coming forth from his pavilion,
> like a champion rejoicing to run his course. (Ps. 19:4-5)

Even more to the point, Paul writes:

Do you not know that in a race all the runners run, but only one gets the prize? Run in such a way as to get the prize. Everyone who competes in the games goes into strict training. They do it to get a crown that will not last; but we do it to get a crown that will last forever. Therefore I do not run like a man running aimlessly; I do not fight like a man beating the air. No, I beat my body and make it my slave so that after I have preached to others, I myself will not be disqualified for the prize. (1 Cor. 9:24-27)

The text from Hebrews 12:1, "Let us run with perseverance the race marked out for us," is a transferable concept. Most of us can align ourselves with a popular sports hero who started out as an underdog (the way most of us see ourselves) and then became a winner. In the 1998 homerun race Sammy Sosa was just as much of a hero as Mark McGwire, though McGwire ended the season with the record. We can identify. We even wear sports teams' logos on our clothing. Competitive sports are transcultural.

MUSIC

Again, no surprises. The church in Africa began to grow 10 percent a year the moment they brought drums into their services of worship. I remember traveling in some of the most remote parts of the world where the only English I heard for weeks was the music of Madonna. How could "Blond Ambition," the "Material Girl," be cross-cultural? Music communicates (albeit by the beat perhaps more than the words). Had I known I was to be an evangelist, I would have taken my mother's advice and stayed with those piano lessons. Oh, to be a Levite. Let me tell you about several experiences.

I've just finished rereading 1 and 2 Chronicles only to be reminded once again of just how crucial music is to the worship of God. Music gathers the people and pleases God. I remember asking God a couple of years ago how King Hezekiah managed to turn a nation of "stiff-necked people" around in less than one generation. Josiah could not do it seventy-five years later—even though they rediscovered the Book of the Law in Josiah's Temple. Then, as I was meditating, I caught a vision. Since I do not consider myself particularly susceptible to visions, when I do have one I tend to remember it. In this instance, I remember the sights, the sounds, and the smells.

I was suddenly outside the Temple in Jerusalem during the latter part of the reign of Hezekiah's father, Ahaz (735–715 B.C.). The nation had been spiritually and morally devastated. Ahaz had not done "what was right in the eyes of the LORD" (2 Chron. 28:1). He had desecrated the Temple with idols, allowed the lamp to go out, and eventually nailed its doors shut.

As the vision continued, I heard people wailing as Ahaz sacrificed Hebrew babies to the pagan god Molech in the Valley of Ben Hinnom, a garbage heap just south of the city. Little wonder that Gehenna (an early word for "hell") literally means "out of the Hinnom."

Then I saw a man and a boy approaching the Temple. It was the prophet Isaiah and Hezekiah—apparently just before Hezekiah became coregent with his father Ahaz. Isaiah, holding to Hezekiah with one hand and a lamp in the other, stopped at the entrance of the Temple, set down the lamp, retrieved a heavy bar from behind "Boaz" (one of the huge bronze pillars), and forced open the Temple doors. I could feel the force of the pounding as the doors were breached. As they entered, all sorts of strange shadows reflected off the pagan images. I heard their feet shuffle across dusty floors. I smelled the musty odor of oil and incense long since left to seep from cracks in ancient jars lining many of the walls and terraces. Then Isaiah led young Hezekiah to the only place not yet desecrated—the Holy of Holies, behind the veil. As they entered, Isaiah whispered, "Hezekiah, just look, don't touch." He then placed Hezekiah prostrate before the ark of the covenant and taught him how to worship God while singing:

> Praise the LORD, O my soul;
>> all my inmost being, praise his holy name.
> Praise the LORD, O my soul,
>> and forget not all his benefits—
> who forgives all your sins
>> and heals all your diseases,
> who redeems your life from the pit
>> and crowns you with love and compassion,
> who satisfies your desires with good things
>> so that your youth is renewed like the eagle's. (Ps. 103:1-5)

Who can doubt the significance of Hezekiah's first acts as king? During the first month of the first year of his reign, he reopened the Temple, cleansed it, and *raised up the priests and Levites*—those responsible for teaching the people how to make music before the Lord.

> Hezekiah assigned the priests and Levites to divisions—each of them according to their duties as priests or Levites—to offer burnt offerings and fellowship offerings, to minister, to give thanks and to sing praises at the gates of the LORD's dwelling.... As the offering began, singing to the LORD began also, accompanied by trumpets and the instruments of David king of Israel. The whole assembly bowed in

worship, while the singers sang and the trumpeters played" (2 Chron. 31:2; 29:27-28).

Hezekiah's reforms brought the entire nation back to God. Want to turn a church around in less than one generation? Worship and music will probably have to play a significant role in the revival.

A few years ago I began attending an independent Pentecostal church on occasion. Although many of the worshipers there were far from Pentecostal in temperament or theology, the place was packed, Sunday after Sunday. Why? Primarily for the music. Some of us know all too well just how boring church can be. I've been to some churches where I had to go home and pray for an hour to get to the place where I was before I went to church. Here, however, the worship was exciting. My daughter would come home saying, "Gee, Dad, that was so much fun I can't wait 'til next Sunday." The worship is lively and relevant. The kids dance, the adults clap, and the band plays on—to the glory of God. There should be no excuse for worship that is boring and irrelevant.

Thirty years ago I served a small church on the south side of Chicago. When I first arrived, only one church in the area was more dead than mine—a huge Roman Catholic edifice around the corner. Less than a dozen people regularly showed up for Mass on Sunday mornings. I assumed that in just a few years the church would die. Then, a few years ago a student of mine asked me to accompany him to a worship service in a church that was making a significant impact on my old neighborhood. More than a little curious, I tagged along. Imagine my surprise: the church we visited—St. Sabina—was the same church that I thought had died years earlier. We arrived at 10:30 A.M. for an 11:00 A.M. service and were fortunate to find a seat. Three and a half hours later the service ended and I still wanted more. This may have been the most significant worship experience that I have had in the past several years. So, what had happened?

A few years earlier a young white priest had been appointed to St. Sabina. He decided to make the church lively and relevant to the community where he lived. Although the people were mostly African American, he carefully "exegeted" (interpreted) the neighborhood, learned the culture, brought it into the church, sanctified it, and then devised models of worship that would communicate. He brought in music and began to recruit the local talent. He learned the "language," adopted two African American children, and involved himself in the lives of those around him by showing compassion and making them feel like winners. Within months people began to attend the various services of worship. Although the revival of St. Sabina is more than music, no one could deny that music is a significant part of what it took to turn a church around in less than one generation. Now, rather than a dozen or so at a single Mass, four different Masses are packed, week after week.

Some years ago several students from Asbury Theological Seminary conceived of a music festival geared to Christian contemporary rock. Within just a few years hundreds had turned into thousands and over the past five years over fifteen thousand young people have streamed annually to Wilmore, Kentucky, for the three-day gathering of people from all over the country. As many as two thousand a night make decisions to follow Jesus Christ.

I recently attended a wedding. At the reception I was particularly interested in one man who seemed bored and uninterested. I felt somewhat concerned until the music started to play. He sang and danced all night.

Music is transcultural.

THE NEED FOR COMMUNITY

People really do need each other. Some of my students have amassed a collection of "Tuttleisms." One of my favorite is far from profound but speaks a terrible truth—"You get singled out; you get picked off." I am personally convinced that the breakup of the family unit (especially among the poor) spawned the gang mentality. People are going to gather in an attempt to survive. We need to belong.

Geese fly in formation because they can fly 70 percent faster and farther in formation than they can on their own. They also swap leadership. They honk to encourage each other. When one can no longer stay with the flock, its mate (for life) drops out with it and remains with it until it recovers or dies. They are on to something.

Richard Leaky's book *People of the Lake* suggests that there were four strains of humankind evolving simultaneously between 1.2 and 1.5 million years ago. The previous theory proposed that the surviving strain is the so-called macho strain—the survival of the fittest. Leaky found, contrary to Darwin, that the "macho" strains were the first to become extinct. Why? They were loners and they got picked off. The only strain to survive to evolve into modern humankind is Homo sapiens. Why? Homo sapiens is the only strain that dared to become community.

Recently a new acquaintance from New York City was describing life in Harlem. He had belonged to a gang there until he was nearly thirty. When I asked, "Why?" he simply laughed, "I had no choice." It seems that to survive on the streets of most inner cities you must belong or you get picked off. Not to belong is to have no one to watch your back. Community is the only way to stay alive. In fact, someone was just in my office who spent the summer working with the so-called counterculture on the West Coast. He reminded me once again that even the counterculture is far more likely to take notice when they realize that Christianity is dead serious about community.

The world over, people are becoming more and more tribal. The recent trends toward nationalism are evidence enough. People want an identity. They want someone to watch their backs. The principle of community is important. Even church youth groups need to develop that kind of mentality. Although I despise the warlike violence that often comes with "protecting the territory," I understand the need for community. My vision for the church is that individual members would so commit to each other that attempts to protect each other in the face of evil and temptation would be fundamental. If you had to reduce the words of Jesus to one sentence (God forbid), it would probably be something like, "Whoever finds his life will lose it, and whoever loses his life for my sake will find it" (Matt. 10:39). The only way to be first is to be last (see Matt. 20:16). The only way to be great is to be a servant (see Matt. 20:26; 23:11). I've always thought that Christians would be heard with authority to the precise degree they were willing to put their lives on the line (see Luke 14:25-27). We call that "radical." Jesus called it "discipleship." The world calls it "survival."

The world over, people gather for protection and meaning. I've observed the kibbutz in Israel. I've seen monasteries in Egypt and Greece. I've spoken with gang warlords on Chicago's Southside, bikers in Australia. I've seen the street children of Brazil. I've particpated in ashrams among Hindus in India. I've seen Buddhist priests gather in Japan, in Korea, and in Thailand. I've watched Taoists in Singapore, Sikhs in Fiji. I've experienced the power of the Muslim community throughout Southeast Asia, Africa, and the Middle East. I've seen gatherings of beggars, the homeless, prostitutes, gays, lesbians, secret societies, all looking for some sort of meaning and protection through community.

The same thing is true in the church. People want spiritual guides, not bureaucrats. They want shepherds, not butchers. Wonderfully, Jesus says:

> "I tell you the truth, I am the gate for the sheep. All who ever came before me were thieves and robbers, but the sheep did not listen to them. I am the gate; whoever enters through me will be saved. He will come in and go out, and find pasture. The thief comes only to steal and kill and destroy; I have come that they may have life, and have it to the full.
>
> "I am the good shepherd. The good shepherd lays down his life for the sheep." (John 10:7-11)

I have always liked this image of the good shepherd who, at night, lays across the threshold of a makeshift pen to protect the sheep.

How can Jesus say "whoever is not against you is for you" (Luke 9:50) and then turn around and say "he who is not with me is against me" (Luke 11:23)? The answer is fairly simple. The first refers to those outside the body. The latter refers to those *within* the body. **Community is so important that those within must protect each other.**

I've always thought it interesting that in Matthew 9 the Pharisees attribute the power of Jesus to the "prince of demons." In this instance, Jesus apparently lets it drop without a challenge. Then, just three chapters later, the same thing happens again. This time, however, Jesus does not let it drop. He goes ballistic, "You brood of vipers, how can you who are evil say anything good?" (Matt. 12:34). So what is going on here? Look at what has taken place in the interim. Jesus has sent out the Twelve. In effect, he is saying, "Mess with me. I'm a dead man headed for a tree. Do not, however, mess with my family!" Jesus closes ranks with his disciples—the community.

Note that community does not always have to be visible. The underground church in the former Soviet countries and in China is an example. I recently journeyed to the Ukraine. There I attended a house church where I prayed with fourteen Christians. None of them had been Christian for more than two months. They had gathered in a small apartment to watch each other's back.

The Spirit of God not only gives us to God but to each other. Although there were people in right relationship with God, there were no Christians prior to Pentecost, because to be a Christian is to be baptized by the Holy Spirit into the body of Christ—a community.

The world without the church will still find its community. Unfortunately, the competition is fierce as the ruler of this world is the devil. Grumble about that if you must, but it is written, "We know that we are children of God, and that the whole world is under the control of the evil one" (1 John 5:19). The good news is that Jesus Christ provides the kind of community that has weapons with "divine power for demolishing strongholds" (2 Cor. 10:4). The church at her best is community. We watch each other's back. Wesley insisted that converts without community are children begotten for the murderer.

The flip side of community is loneliness. Since the need for community is universal, then those without a significant community are vulnerable. Interestingly, loneliness is rarely the result of our not knowing others. Usually it is the result of others not knowing us, and usually others do not know us because we do not want to be known. Furthermore, we do not want to be known because we do not trust. We are afraid of revealing who we are and making ourselves vulnerable to still more abuse.

For more than a decade, at least three times a year I took six to eight students into local churches to lead a "Faith Renewal Weekend." The primary objective was to create community. At the conclusion of the first night, we divided the entire congregation into groups of threes. I asked them to answer three simple questions among themselves and then to pray for each other, out loud if possible, though we would settle for silent prayer. With this simple exercise I saw pre-Christians lead pre-Christians to Christ. The three questions? (1) Tell your name and something interesting about yourself. (2) What one thing has been an encouragement to you over the past two weeks to a month? (3) What one thing would you like for God to do for you this weekend? Admittedly, none of that sounds terribly profound, but the need to share is transcultural.

Obviously the church is the place where that kind of trust should be most available. Unfortunately, that is not always the case. The accusation that "we shoot our own wounded" is sometimes true. George Bernard Shaw said, "Leave Christians alone, they'll kill each other." God forbid! Surely the church has more to offer than the local tavern. (Some years ago Dan Quayle became weary of the immorality seemingly celebrated in the television show *Murphy Brown,* while I was just as weary of the sniveling camaraderie portrayed in *Cheers.*)

"Let them know we are Christians by our love" is more than lyrics to a campfire song. The church at her best has no equal for meeting the world's most basic needs. When we love one another, establishing vital community is what we are all about. Little wonder the author of the letter to the Hebrews exhorts: "Let us not give up meeting together, as some are in the habit of doing, but let us encourage one another—and all the more as you see the Day approaching" (Heb. 10:25).

I am convinced that the church will attract the unchurched to the precise degree that it models community. People survive and then thrive only in community.

AN INTERNAL DIMENSION

So far our focus has been primarily on the external. The principles of a transcultural presentation of the gospel, however, have internal dimensions as well. In fact, it is the internal dimension that most effectively establishes the appeal to the gospel and provides the most important principle for a gospel presentation that is truly transcultural. Although my dinner party friend shared at least some enthusiasm for all of the areas of interest discussed above, this internal dimension provided the key.

51

CHAPTER FIVE

The Key

Now we are ready for the key that turns the lock. A trans-cultural gospel must contain a concept that makes a cross-cultural appeal to the gospel of Jesus Christ. Not surprisingly, my neighborhood friend from the dinner party confirmed the key. In spite of a life that seemed self-contained, one evening as we visited he confessed, "The good news you talk about does have its appeal. If I were ever to become a Christian, it would be in an attempt to change some things that have nagged at me for years. You speak of power. I could use some of that."

Some days later we met for lunch. Over bowls of clam chowder I told him this story.

THE MAN IN BANGKOK

Several years ago, in the midst of one of my travels, I journeyed to Thailand. After a few days I was depressed. The country seemed troubled. The people seemed hopeless. Amidst magnificent palaces and beautiful shrines was incredible poverty. Thirty percent of the women in Thailand between the ages of 18 and 30 are prostitutes and 80 percent of those have AIDS. One Sunday I was looking for a place to worship. As I walked the streets of Bangkok, I saw a young Thai carrying a Bible. I approached him and asked directions to any of the local churches. He seemed friendly and smiled. After introducing himself (his name was Prayong), somewhat to my surprise he offered to direct me personally. Although I was a bit uneasy with my willingness to trust this total stranger, the two of us headed off, winding endlessly through narrow lanes and passageways. As we walked, this young man told me an interesting story.

Prayong had been raised a Buddhist in Chiang Mai, a beautiful city in the far north of the country. As a small boy he had experienced the usual pressures to succeed. His parents, as was common to Asian cultures, expected him to excel in school. Try as he might, he could never become more than an average student. Tragically, in his shame, he had eventually turned to drugs and alcohol as an escape.

Some years later he had made several attempts to sober up. His first instinct was to use willpower. He was unsuccessful. He was powerless. Next, he turned to the religion of his youth. The Buddhist philosophy told him what to do, but not how to do it. Again, he was unsuccessful. He was powerless.

Desperate and alone he stumbled one night into the home of a friend. There he was introduced to a Christian missionary who happened to be visiting. Almost contemptuously, Prayong challenged the missionary to help him overcome his addiction. Within days he was not only sober, but back at work and in school. As I listened to the account of his conversion, I was captivated. I wanted to know more. I pressed him for further details. In a quiet and unassuming way he described his deliverance. Listen to the key.

THE NEED TO OVERCOME

The missionary had explained to Prayong that his dilemma was not uncommon. Although everyone was not dependent upon drugs and alcohol, at some point everyone was a slave to something and felt powerless to overcome. Inexplicably, Prayong felt hope. As Prayong pondered, the missionary shared the following passage, which Prayong remembered as being most critical.

This is love for God: to obey his commands. And his commands are not burdensome, for everyone born of God *overcomes* the world. This is the victory that has *overcome* the world, even our faith. Who is it that *overcomes* the world? Only he who believes that Jesus is the Son of God. (1 John 5:3-5, emphasis added)

Although Prayong did not believe in God (his Buddhist philosophy had never prepared him for such belief), he had heard of Jesus and was curious. He was receptive. Let me use his own words: "I had become so frustrated with my inability *to measure up* to the expectations of my parents, I was desperate to turn my life around and was ready to listen."

The missionary explained that Christians believe that there is a God, the Creator of the universe, who loves and cares for them and who makes a power available to sustain them through their struggles. Prayong then recalled the missionary quoting the following passages (also from 1 John) as significant: "The whole world is under the control of the evil one" (5:19), but "the one who is in you is greater than the one who is in the world" (4:4). He was "hooked." He had nothing to lose. When the missionary challenged him to put his faith and trust in Jesus Christ as Savior and Lord so that he might know the power of God to overcome, Prayong said, "Yes." Suddenly he experienced a rush! The power of the Holy Spirit filled him with faith, and hope, and love. He described it like this, "I was immediately sober. Within the week I had gone back to school and within the month was near the top of my class."

This man's witness rang true. I was impressed and still wanted to hear more. We approached a small building with a cross above its door. As we entered a room filled with people singing, Prayong led me to a seat and walked immediately to the pulpit. Imagine my surprise when he opened his Bible and began to preach. He was an evangelist. He preached a marvelous sermon on "The Prodigal Son."

After the church service, Prayong and I spent the better part of the afternoon together. I took notes and later that evening recorded these thoughts in my journal.

A UNIVERSAL OUGHTNESS

Within everyone (except perhaps for the lonely sociopath) there is some form of oughtness—a moral, ethical, or even religious form of *law* where people (as with Prayong) feel the need to measure up to some standard, some cultural imperative. Paul writes:

> When Gentiles, who do not have the law, do by nature things required by the law, they are a law for themselves, even though they do not have the law, since they show that the requirements of the law are written on their hearts, their consciences also bearing witness, and their thoughts now accusing, now even defending them. (Rom. 2:14-15)

This concept is a bit more sophisticated than Kant's "categorical imperative," or even Calvin's "common grace," and I have found this oughtness strong enough in many (especially among those who are serious about things eternal) that they are receptive to the gospel.

Permit me to expand on this last sentence. Do not get bored. This can help you. The German philosopher Immanuel Kant insisted that basic to the nature of humankind is an instinctive need—an inward necessity—to measure up to those laws that are confirmed by an impulse common to everyone. In his *Critique of Pure Reason* he calls this inherent drive *a priori* (as opposed to *a posteriori*, or empirical knowledge taken from experience). *A priori* propositions (independent from acquired or learned experience) are axioms of intuition—an innate curiosity—that motivate all of life.

In theological terms, John Calvin referred to a similar drive resulting from what he calls "common grace." Again, instinctive to our nature as God's creation, everyone has some *natural* inclination to seek what is good and to reject what is bad.

Interestingly, John Wesley gives this same impulse a different twist. Wesley insisted that Calvin "took free will too far." Wesley argued that there was nothing inherently good within us, but that God, by the Holy Spirit, had *supernaturally* imbued everyone with the desire to know God. Let me now relate this to the transcultural presentation of the gospel.

56

RELEVANCE FOR THE GOSPEL

Since that day spent with my young Thai friend, Prayong, I have tested this principle of a universal need to measure up to some form of oughtness hundreds of times.

As I concluded the story of Prayong, I could feel the conversation with my neighborhood friend turn even more serious. He seemed concerned. I decided simply to listen to him. After nearly thirty years in the firm he had helped to establish he was being forced into early retirement. After being turned out of what he did best, what could he do now? He was too young just to go fishing or work in the yard for the rest of his life. He still wanted his life to count for something. How could those whom he helped to succeed now turn on him with comments such as "You no longer project the company image. Your particular expertise can now be better served by younger people who do not command an executive salary. It is purely a question of economics." The obligatory watch left him cold and resentful. I could understand why. I continued to listen for nearly an hour. As we left the restaurant, I hugged him but said nothing. Still, I knew that God was at work in him, and, for the first time perhaps, my friend and I had really communicated.

Significant to sharing the gospel is that whenever (and almost without exception) I have found those who were dead serious about knowing God (and sometimes their understanding of God was no more sophisticated than a curiosity about the unknown), they had become frustrated with their inability to measure up to this oughtness and were open and responsive to the good news of the power of the Holy Spirit available through faith in Jesus Christ. There was always a need to measure up.

Kant, you remember, in his *Critique of Pure Reason* argued that "pure reason" was *a priori*, or inherent, built upon general truths, and bearing the character of inward necessity. My contention here is that there is a presentation of the gospel that is *a priori*, or inherent, built upon general truths, and bearing the character of inward necessity for every culture. This "categorical imperative," this "universal ought-ness," is the bedrock of a transcultural gospel.

There is an interesting aside to all of this that is critical for sharing the good news of Jesus Christ. As one might suspect, Calvin's "common grace" is not sufficient for salvation. A "special grace" (which, according to Calvin, was *limited* to the "elect" and also *irresistible*) must be added to this common grace in order for honest seekers to respond to the claims of the gospel upon their lives. In other words, although this oughtness is at work in everyone, it accomplishes nothing by itself. God has somehow chosen (quite apart from our own response) who will be saved and who will be lost.

The Swiss theologian Karl Barth, arguably the greatest theologian in this century, made a reasonable attempt to rescue this doctrine of election—or predestination—from its perniciousness. He insisted that God has not elected or chosen individuals but that God has chosen Jesus Christ and that salvation is to identify, by faith, with "the elect man Jesus." Salvation is for those who are baptized by the Holy Spirit into the body of Christ. Barth, therefore, retained the biblical aspects of the doctrine of election (see Rom. 8:28-30) while maintaining an evangelistic appeal to faith in Jesus Christ (see John 3:16).

Perhaps even more significant to our purposes here is that two hundred years before Barth, John Wesley objected to Calvin's limited and irresistible "special grace" by insisting that "prevenient grace" (roughly analogous to Calvin's special grace) was *universal* and *resistible*. For Wesley, although this universal oughtness was not inherent, the effect was the same. That same oughtness was simply the universal work of the Holy Spirit.

On several occasions I have tested this principle among some of the other religions of the world. They all have that universal drive to measure up. Hinduism, for example, grapples with the nature of self. One of the Hindu saints, Tukuram, wrote this poem:

> As on the bank the poor fish lies
> And gasps and writhes in pain,
> Or as a man with anxious eyes
> Seeks hidden gold in vain,—
> So is my heart distressed and cries
> To come to thee again
> Have mercy.[1]

1. Tukuram followed the path of Bhakti (intense devotion). Quoted in an unpublished paper by Peg Ulmet.

Buddhism struggles with the nature and cause of suffering. Islam seeks ways to submit to Allah, the Almighty Creator. Primal religions, by and large, battle evil spirits. All religions have some insatiable need to fulfill a (usually someone else's) concept of what it means to be "spiritual."

In review, the relevance of all this for our sharing of the gospel is that people the world over have a need (whether inherent or by the work of the Holy Spirit) to fulfill some form of law and have become frustrated with their inability to measure up. Whether Kant's "categorical imperative," or Calvin's "common grace" (especially as interpreted by Barth), or Wesley's "prevenient grace," the result is the same, this universal oughtness and the subsequent need for power to measure up is transcultural. Thus, this principle is basic to my search for a transcultural gospel.

In the next chapter we will put this key together with additional clues from other transcultural common denominators (some of which we have already discussed) in an attempt to create a working tool for faith-sharing among pre-Christians, especially in cross-cultural settings.

CHAPTER SIX

A Transcultural Gospel

Let's begin this chapter with a reminder. The presentation here is not a formula. We have already established that no single approach (especially in cross-cultural settings) will communicate the gospel. The intent here is to provide some tools for establishing dynamic, multidimensional principles for a transcultural presentation of the gospel. Although the individual concepts are not self-contained (they are incomplete in and of themselves), I want you to be able to take these principles and use them, *in any order,* to communicate the good news of Jesus Christ. Remember, the result, although a step beyond so-called pre-evangelism, is simply prerequisite to the more detailed presentation of the gospel later on, usually in community.

THE PRINCIPLES

Let me reiterate that although the list below might imply some logical progression, this is not a linear (straight line) approach. As will be demonstrated in the next chapter, if you *understand the concepts,* the order of presentation should reveal itself within the context of an evangelistic encounter. Patience usually reveals that when one door opens, they all open. Here are the principles:

People the world over have a need

- to measure up to some form of law.
- to understand their origin.
- to overcome temptation.
- to experience community.

I will now expand upon these principles in order to explain the concepts more fully. Realize that your own explanation of these principles will be different from mine. That is as it should be. We all look at things differently. I always tell my students, "I'm not out to clone anyone. My theology cannot hold a candle to your theology in your own sphere of influence." The material below should serve only as a catalyst for your own work to follow.

THE NEED TO MEASURE UP

In our last chapter we noted that the key to a transcultural gospel is the need to measure up to some form of law at work within all of us, the world over.

Imagine meeting someone for the first time in a cross-cultural setting (at home or abroad). The opportunity for conversation presents itself. Since I genuinely like people and find most of them interesting, my approach is usually to begin by listening, and then to ask questions. I rarely begin with an evangelistic agenda. I'm not looking to force an opening where I can speak that definitive word for God. I believe that evangelism is first of all God's agenda, not mine, and when (or if) God opens the door, I want to be caring and sensitive enough to walk through it. Several of my students once pointed out that they had never heard me volunteer any information about myself until I was asked. I was a bit surprised that they had noticed, but realized that in most cases this is true. Although I could illustrate this with many different experiences, let me share with you just one, and then, for the sake of continuity in demonstrating our principles, build upon this story throughout the rest of the chapter.

Some years ago I boarded a plane for a short flight from Chicago to Detroit. I desperately needed to grade some papers that I had promised to hand back to my students upon my return. I was in no mood for conversation. As I approached my seat, I noticed a woman in the one next to mine. As she introduced herself, it was apparent to me, "This woman wants to talk." Without wanting to be rude, I simply acknowledged her greeting, immediately opened my briefcase, and began reading one of the papers. If I could just get started (or so I thought), I was probably safe. Somewhat to my surprise, within seconds she asked, "What are you doing?" Without looking up, I mumbled, "Grading papers." She asked again, "Oh, what do you teach?" I said (this time more clearly), "Theology." She seemed even more curious, "That's interesting. Where do you teach?" I said, "Oral Roberts University." Then she asked, "Where's that? I've never heard of Oral Roberts University." For some reason I responded, "Have you ever heard of Oral Roberts?" "No," she easily admitted. Now *I* was curious, so I put the paper away, turned to her, and said just four words, "Tell me about yourself."

For the next thirty minutes she told me about herself. She lived with her family in a beautiful house on the North Shore of Chicago. Her husband had a terrific job. Her children were doing well in school. Her life seemed wonderful. I found myself listening with interest, saying almost nothing. Then, without warning, her story shifted. Almost without my realizing it, she was no longer telling me how wonderful her life was; she was telling how miserable she was. No matter how hard she tried, she could not measure up to the expectations of family and friends. In spite of what first appeared to be an almost idyllic life, she was frustrated and in the depths of despair.

At this point, the plane was still on the runway and the pilot announced that mechanical trouble would delay our departure. Although I had still said almost nothing, the door was open. For the next two hours (much of the detail will be shared below) we talked about a God who loves and the power of the Holy Spirit made available through faith and trust in Jesus Christ. During the landing in Detroit, she asked, "What's to prevent me from accepting Jesus Christ, right now?" I said, "Don't unbuckle your safety belt. You're not leaving this airplane until we pray." My papers did not get graded, but she found peace.

So, what's the point? Frustration breeds despair. It has been suggested that we can spend forty days without food but not a single day without hope. Some expectation of a positive future is absolutely essential to survive. This woman, like so many people around the world, was miserable because she felt utterly hopeless in her attempts to live up to expectations. Although in this instance the "law" that had crippled her was hardly religious, it opened the door to the gospel of Jesus Christ. The result? **The grace of God redefined her expectations and gave her hope for the future.** Let's linger for a moment on this last sentence before moving on to the next principle.

Sometimes the goals and expectations that lead to frustration are unreasonable—totally unrealistic. Would God empower us to live up to goals that are non-Christian (at best) or anti-Christian (at worst)? Of course not. Since the frustration that opens the door—the despair over an inability to measure up—is sometimes the result of unreasonable goals, once in the room, God must rearrange the furniture. The law, empowered by the gospel, must conform to the Word of God. Be encouraged, that law is reasonable—totally realistic. These words of Jesus have this in mind:

> Come to me, all you who are weary and burdened, and I will give you rest. Take my yoke upon you and learn from me, for I am gentle and humble in heart, and you will find rest for your souls. For my yoke is easy and my burden is light. (Matt. 11:28-30)

The apostle Paul places this same principle within the context of temptation:

> No temptation has seized you except what is common to man. And God is faithful; he will not let you be tempted beyond what you can bear. But when you are tempted, he will also provide a way out so that you can stand up under it. (1 Cor. 10:13)

Again, although the expectations that lead to despair may be unreasonable, the grace of God redefines those expectations and empowers us to measure up to goals that promise freedom and peace. Once my friend on the plane understood this, she experienced a hope that led her to faith in Jesus Christ. The remaining principles will describe what we talked about during those two hours of sharing after the door had been opened.

UNDERSTANDING ONE'S ORIGIN

Sometimes in an evangelistic encounter the need to measure up is present but unspoken. Even though no direct reference is made, I can sense the frustration and know that the principle is already at work. In those instances, since there is no need to belabor the issue, I frequently begin by talking about "the power to overcome," or, as in the present illustration, by talking about a God who loves and cares and *then* creates.

Notice the emphasis upon the word "then." Although many people around the world have little or no understanding of God, they do have an innate curiosity about their origin. Some adopted children seek out their biological parents, but the even bigger issue is creation. That is *a priori,* a given. In order to understand creation fully, however, it is essential to place it within the context of love.

My seatmate on the plane knew almost nothing about God. She had never attended church (except for weddings and funerals); she apparently lived in a purely secular world (talk about cross-cultural); yet she had a curiosity about her own beginning. Once the door had been opened by her frustration over an inability to measure up, this is where we began. *She* actually set the agenda. I remember one of her first questions, "So, where do we come from?"

For quite some time we talked about the God of the Bible, not as an "It" but as one who loves and cares and who wants to be known. Before time began, however, God was alone. To be known would require creation—someone who could respond. This presented a problem. Genuine response demands freedom—the freedom to accept or reject. If we could not say no, our yes would be meaningless. So, from the beginning, God (knowing all things) knew full well that to create humankind (and a universe in which to live) would invite rebellion. God knew that we would be tempted, break fellowship, and alienate ourselves—without hope in the world. The angels would do it. Men, women, and children would do it. That was the dilemma. So, how could a fallen creation be redeemed? How could sin and death (the price of the Fall) be overcome? God had a plan.

The Bible teaches that God has one essence (the Shema in Deuteronomy 6:4 states that the Lord our God is *one* God) but is manifested in three distinct persons—Father, Son, and Holy Spirit (Matt. 28:19). There is no analogy that can adequately explain this (I am told that heresy is born when little minds try to solve big paradoxes). For years I used the example of water as liquid, ice, and steam. Water, whether heated or frozen, is still H_2O. This was more helpful for some than for others. So, I continued to search for a way of describing the Triune God anticipating the fall of creation and its ultimate redemption.

Then, late one night, I caught an image. As I studied the earlier chapters in the book of Genesis, I imagined the three persons of the Trinity discussing the dilemma of creation. I watched and listened as they talked among themselves, like someone with multiple personalities. That part of God that we call Father was the first to speak. "We want to be known. We will create man and woman in our own image (see Gen. 1:26), and we will love them like children." The Son replied, "Will they love us back?" Then I heard the voice of the Spirit, like wind blowing in trees, "As we become known, some of them will love us back, because we will be merciful and kind. In spite of their rebellion, our compassion will lead them to repentance and faith."

Then, as they continued to contemplate Creation and the Fall, their voices dropped. There was a catch. It became painfully apparent that in order to be known fully and to guarantee salvation, one of them would have to visit and redeem the people (see Luke 1:68). One of them would have to become flesh and dwell among them (see John 1:14). Consistent with the nature of covenant, a sacrifice would be required, since "without the shedding of blood there is no forgiveness" of sins (Heb. 9:22). Furthermore, since humanity has fallen, this sacrifice would have to be human and without blemish (see Heb. 10:1-4). Since all of creation would sin and fall short of the glory of God (see Rom. 3:23), only the one sent could fulfill such a sacrifice.

Suddenly, I imagined the Son stepping forward to be chosen by the

Father as the one who would go (1 Peter 1:20). He spoke, "Send me. 'I will declare your name to my brothers; in the presence of the congregation I will sing your praises' (Heb. 2:12). I will share in their humanity so that by my death I might destroy him who will hold the power of death—that is the devil—and free those who all their lives have been held in slavery (see Heb. 2:14-15). Make me like them in every respect so that I might be 'a merciful and faithful high priest' in your service, that I 'might make atonement for the sins of the people.' Then, because I too have suffered and been tempted, I will be able 'to help those who are being tempted' (see Heb. 2:17-18). They will know that we love them, not because we imagine how they feel when they hurt inside, but because we know how they feel when they hurt inside, because I have been there."

So, even before God created, it was decided. The price of creation would require the death of the Son. Even though that Son would then be raised from the dead in order to demonstrate God's victory over sin and death (no small thing), it was an incredible price to pay.

As I sat with my friend on the plane, I could sense her response. She was beginning to realize the love and care God has for all of creation. The words from John 3:16, "For God so loved the world that he gave his one and only Son, that whoever believes in him shall not perish but have eternal life," were beginning to make sense.

The door had been opened, and I began with where she was—an interest in her own beginning. I then pointed out (as we have already noted) that God was a Redeemer before God was a Creator. God loved before God made. This was crucial for her understanding. She was now ready for the appeal.

OVERCOMING TEMPTATION

Frustration and lack of power to overcome provided the catalyst for faith in Jesus Christ. If you ever want to get someone's attention, try this for an opening: "Have you ever wanted to change but lacked the power to overcome that which separates you from God, yourself, and those around you? Then listen to this!" I can almost guarantee some interest—at least for thirty seconds. Then you had better start to deliver. I had her attention. Now it was time to deliver. Fear not. If the gospel is true, then it is God who delivers, through faith in Jesus Christ—God's provision for our sin.

In the eternal perspective, Christianity makes sense. Since children are transcultural, the gift of a Son provided immediate identification for my airplane seatmate. She was into this. I could tell. As she thought about her own children, she marveled at God's willingness to sacrifice a Son. It was equally important for her to realize that it was our own sin that led to Jesus' death. At one point she shook her head, "How could God forgive us for that?" I added, "Not only does God forgive us for the death of the Son; God wants us to share in the inheritance of his glory—eternal life. From the world's point of view, that makes God insane. From our point of view, that makes God's love real." We then began to talk about power.

I knew it was important for her to understand that there was hope. She did not have to wallow in her own impotence any longer. **She needed to know about the Holy Spirit.** Carefully, I began to explain that if she was willing for God to take her sin from her and to place her faith and trust in Jesus Christ (even as she was trusting the airline to get her to Detroit), then God would fill her with the Holy Spirit and empower her to overcome. She could actually measure up to a law that would bring fulfillment and peace.

For years now I have lectured about the analogy between wind and Spirit. The Old Testament word for wind (in the Hebrew, *ruah*) is translated by the New Testament word for spirit (in the Greek, *pneuma*). Wind equals spirit and spirit equals wind. That is no accidental metaphor. Meteorologists tell us that wind moves from high pressure to low pressure, the point of least resistance. Low pressure cells over bodies of water can attract wind at more than two hundred miles an hour. It is terribly significant that the Spirit, like wind, moves from high pressure to low pressure, the point of least resistance. Giving up on our own righteousness—the essence of repentance—and placing our faith and trust in the righteousness of Jesus Christ—a faithful and merciful high priest—creates low pressure. Just as one does not have to convince wind to move from high pressure to low pressure (that's what wind does), one does not have to convince the

Spirit to move from high pressure to low pressure (that's what the Spirit does). Consequently, salvation (and basic spirituality for that matter) is not so much "grunt and groan" as **repent and believe.**

I felt that this concept was so important that I went back to it several times. I began talking about *repentance.* One of my seminary professors used to say that repentance is the point of the Spirit's sword. Many cultures, however, have no understanding of repentance. So, what is repentance and how does it work?

Repentance is a willingness for God to take from us the sin in our lives—those things that separate us from God, from ourselves, and from those around us (including, of course, the basic elements of our natural environment). If it is not separating us from God, ourselves, and those around us, stop worrying about it. There is enough real guilt in all of us without our having to make it up. Notice that I said a *willingness* for God to take from us. I have heard repentance defined in most Christian circles as turning one's back on sin—an about-face. In truth, that is easier said than done. In fact, it is impossible. Just try to take your eyes off sin. It will eat your lunch. You will have ghastly thoughts in the midst of the Lord's Prayer. It will consume you twenty-four hours a day. Again, Christian repentance is a willingness (as far as we know our own hearts) for God to take our sin from us, who then, by the Holy Spirit, moves from high pressure to low pressure, bearing witness with our spirits that we are children of God—the essence of faith—and empowering us to overcome.

Although I sensed that at one point she was drifting off, I simply nudged her and smiled, "Don't you dare get bored. Stay with me! This is important." I continued to explain that repentance that leads to faith in Christ alone—the "yes," the "I give up on my own righteousness and place my faith and trust in the righteousness of Christ"—creates low pressure. The Holy Spirit who is at work drawing people the world over—God's initiative in the drama of rescue—no longer woos, but rushes to the very core of our being, creating and re-creating after the mind of Christ. She asked me to explain.

I asked her to imagine cause and effect. Again, if our response is repentance (our "initiative" to God's initiative), then God's response is the gift of faith through the indwelling power of the Holy Spirit (see Rom. 8:16, John Wesley's favorite text), what I sometimes refer to as the "swoosh." The swoosh, however, is *fact*, not *feeling*. I cautioned her, "Do not look for some emotional charge and do not be misled by the terms 'cause' and 'effect.' The cause, as well as the effect, is enabled by God's grace."

What might not have been obvious from the dialogue above is the role of the Holy Spirit in all of this. Since the Fall—the sin of Adam and Eve (never once did she ask whether or not this story was to be taken literally, and believe me, I never pressed the point)—our first forebears lost their ability to perceive reality beyond the senses. They became mortal, locked into a five-dimensional world bound by height, width, depth, time, and motion. As a result, it was necessary for God to level the playing field. Even before the coming of the Son, the Holy Spirit entered the world, acting upon all of us from the moment of our conception, guaranteeing our freedom to say "yes" once we understand the claims of the gospel upon our lives. In other words, first God woos us (the work of the Spirit), then provides a sacrifice for our sin (the work of the Son), then calls us to repentance and faith and empowers us to measure up, so that our relationship with God is renewed. Notice, God does not save us and then say, "Okay, I've saved you, now live up to it." God saves us and then empowers us to overcome those things that would attempt to swallow us. That is the continuing work of the Spirit. This work usually takes place in community.

THE IMPORTANCE OF COMMUNITY

For thirty years I have refused to talk about the gospel without some reference to the larger perspective of follow-up, sometimes referred to as discipleship.

Although our emphasis here has been on the initial response (and this section will be all too brief), we need to ask the question, "Born again, what then?" The real work of evangelism is brought to fruition when Christians are gathered and strengthened in their newfound faith, usually in community. In fact, evangelism can begin in community. I've just finished reading *How the Irish Saved Civilization*.[1] It is

1. *How the Irish Saved Civilization*, Thomas Cahill, ed. (New York: Doubleday, 1995).

interesting that the Celtic way of evangelism was not to convert and then to join, but to join and then to convert within the context of a fellowship of believers. George Hunter has just completed a new book that describes this Celtic approach in some detail.[2]

One of my problems with the Four Spiritual Laws of Campus Crusade for Christ is the lack of emphasis upon community. We already established that "to get singled out is to get picked off." Fortunately, salvation not only gives us to God, it gives us to each other. Again, years ago I promised myself that I would always direct each new convert to the next level of commitment and to a community of believers. It would amaze you how God opens those doors.

Just last month I talked with a telephone agent who was assigning me a new number. I was in Kentucky; she was in Florida. God opened a door and in twenty minutes she (to use her own words) had "an encounter with the living God," right there over the phone. Within blocks of her home was a church where I knew and trusted the pastors. I simply called the church, spoke with one of the pastors, gave him her number, and he followed up immediately. She is now being cared for by a community of believers.

John Wesley insisted that he would far rather retain than gain. Late in the Revival, he refused to preach in the open air if there was not already a Society in place who could encourage and instruct those being saved.

So, what is so important about community? We previously established that the need to belong in order to survive is transcultural. Community is where we make contact with other Christians. A recent book entitled *The Blessing* describes the need for affection, the need to be affirmed, the need to be "valued" by family and friends, the need for commitment—to others and for others—among those who are important in our lives. Trust me, this need is constant, from cradle to grave.

Community is where we come into physical contact with those of like mind and spirit. It is (or should be) a safe place to be touched. I am told that each hand has 1.5 million receptors. Our hands were created for healing and nurture. We all know that babies will not survive

---

2. A book entitled, *The Celtic Way of Evangelism: How Christianity Can Reach the West ... Again,* to be published by Abingdon Press in 2000.

without some kind of touch. Appropriate touching and holding communicate caring. Over the years, all of my children have sent me this message. When they need attention, how many times have I heard them say, "Daddy, feel my head and see if I have a fever."

Recent studies tell us that the highest suicide rate in America is among people of Asian descent. In an Asian culture, nuclear families (mothers and fathers) evaluate (and evaluation to the extreme becomes rejection); they drive their children to excel. It is the extended families (aunts, uncles, grandparents) that affirm and provide the "unconditional" love. Outside the Asian context and apart from their extended families where affirmation is available, those from an Asian culture frequently despair. The church must take up the slack. A warm, caring, affirming community is absolutely necessary.

So, what about my seatmate on the plane? Would it surprise you to learn that I just so happened to have a former student with a church in her neighborhood? Their daughters went to school together. As we walked up the exit ramp I noticed a bank of telephones on the opposite wall. I immediately called my former student and introduced them over the phone. They made plans to meet together upon her return. She was into a Bible study within the week. She learned how to pray. She got involved, not only in the church but in the neighborhood as well. Her ministry is an absolute inspiration to me. It serves me right.

A CHALLENGE

Although the encounter with the woman on the plane seems almost too "pat" to be true, let me assure you that opportunities for these kinds of experiences are all around us. That is not to imply that every opportunity is this rewarding. Some of my feeble attempts have been rejected outright. On some occasions I've been ridiculed and even cursed.

In a book published more than twenty-five years ago I told the story of a man in prison. As the pastor of a local church it was my practice to visit the county jail one afternoon a week. Someone would push a pillow through the bars so that I could sit on the floor and speak to the men about faith in God. After weeks of sharing with them, one of the men who had resisted me the most suddenly accepted Christ. I was thrilled. The next day I went to see my new convert, just to polish him up a bit. He met me at the bars and said something I will never forget, "Tuttle, I laid awake all last night, thinking. Suddenly it occurred to me that it takes an average of twenty-five different witnesses before any real encounter with God takes place and just because you were number twenty-five, you think you did it all, and you stink." He had me. I began to weep. Just because I was number twenty-five I thought I had done it all, when twenty-four, just as important, had gone before me. Come on reader, do you believe that? I wish some of my evangelical friends would live like it!

How many times do we share the gospel, receive no apparent response, and go home and pout, "I blew it." I am always exhorting my students, "Numbers one to twenty-four are just as important as number twenty-five." This might be a bit of an oversimplification, but it takes twenty-four no's to get a yes. That means that inherent to evangelism is twenty-four times more rejections than affirmations. Most of us resist evangelism because we fear rejection. Get over it! Don't take it so personally. If we understand the work of the Spirit, we should be just as affirmed by being numbers one to twenty-four as by being number twenty-five.

Most mornings I include in my daily prayers, "God, make me sensitive to my opportunities for ministry." **Let me give you a challenge.** Pray that prayer. It will open doors you never dreamed possible. Know that rejection is going to happen. It is inevitable, so do not let it defeat you. Just remember, **God has more invested in your ministry than you do.** God takes the initiative in the drama of rescue. Be you "doctor, lawyer, or Indian chief," even as you read these words, the Spirit of God is already at work, preparing people the world over for your ministry within your sphere of influence.

Remember my friend from the dinner party? The next time we met he eagerly wanted to talk about God. With simply a gentle prod he was able to identify people who had influenced him for God, mostly without his even being aware of the impact. From his experience of known Christians he remembered his mother's love and care. He told me about the cheerfulness of a laborer on one of his job sites. There was a secretary who was always eager to please, a client who cared about his employees, even a lawyer who wanted to do the right thing in some rather sticky legal matters that would affect a building project.

Then as he continued to talk it was apparent that all of the principles were at work. It was obvious to me that he still felt powerless to measure up. He was innately curious about his own origin. He was becoming more and more curious about a God who wants to be known, who loves and then creates. He was not yet ready for faith in Jesus Christ, but he was asking questions about the power of the Holy Spirit available to overcome that which was keeping him from a more meaningful life. I began to pray that he would find the kind of community that would lead him to faith, sustain him in his walk with God, and then bind him to others who would watch his back. He was not just my neighbor, he was now my friend. I wanted his hope renewed. Still, I had to be patient. We continued to communicate.

It is time now to demonstrate the power of a transcultural gospel in actual case studies. The results of bearing witness to these principles will absolutely amaze you. Here are some examples.

CHAPTER SEVEN

The Principles Applied: The Case Studies

The following case studies are intended to illustrate a presentation of the gospel that uses all of the principles demonstrated in the previous chapter. All of them happened just as they are told. Note especially the order in which the principles are shared. Although each case is somewhat abbreviated, the necessary cross-cultural ingredients of content and flexibility should become apparent.

TAK ON THE PLANE FROM KIEV TO PARIS

I first saw Tak on a bus to the airport in Kiev. He looked to be a middle-aged Asian businessman. I was a bit tired after a two-week mission trip to the Ukraine with students from seminary, so I was dozing. Then I noticed a weary young woman who had boarded the bus in an attempt to sell some of her art. As she was showing us several paintings, asking fifteen dollars for each, I remember thinking to myself, "These are good, but not great." Although she appeared somewhat shy, within minutes she approached the Asian businessman. I overheard him say as he examined one particular painting, "This is not worth fifteen dollars," (a month's wage in the former

Soviet Republic), "it must be worth at least two hundred and fifty dollars. I'll give you two hundred and fifty dollars for it." I saw this woman instantly transformed before my eyes. As the businessman gave her the money, she beamed. I was liking this guy already, a lot!

In the airport I had to spend time with my students, making sure that they were ready for the flight to Paris, which boarded in less than an hour. When I finally had time to sit down and reflect, I found myself praying for the woman who had sold the painting and for the man who had bought it. When I looked up the businessman was standing in line in front of me, the painting under his arm. As I caught his eye, our flight was called, so all I managed to do was smile and nod.

On the plane I was pleased to find the seat next to mine empty. As we took off, I took out my Bible to catch up on some reading. After a few minutes, I was beginning to nod so I closed my eyes and stretched out for a brief nap. Suddenly, I felt the cushion in the seat next to me sink as someone sat down. As I opened one eye, he spoke. "We need to talk." It was the Asian businessman. I said, somewhat surprised, since he obviously knew nothing about me, "About what?" He said, "I don't know. I just know we have to talk." I said, "So, talk."

As he began to speak, I could see several of my students scattering to the back of the plane, no doubt to pray. His name was Tak, and he owned several businesses in London but lived just north of Oxford. Before I could respond further, he began telling me an interesting story.

He was the oldest son of a man dying in a hospital in Japan. On Friday (this was Monday) he was flying to Tokyo to see a father to whom he had not spoken in over ten years. It seems that his father had taken a mistress when Tak was in university, and when his mother had discovered the affair, she died within months, grieved and humiliated. Subsequently, Tak and his father had been alienated. Since his father married the mistress after his mother's death, Tak, angry and depressed, refused even to visit the family home. As the oldest son, however, he knew that he and his father had to be reconciled before his father's death. He explained that in an Asian culture this was most important. I asked, "What would it take?" He said, "A miracle." Thinking we were on to something, I asked, "Do you believe in miracles?" He laughed, "Of course not. I don't even believe in God."

76

Then, again before I could respond further, he said something even more interesting, "My mother was Buddhist and a saint. Since she died, I have no one to admire." Without so much as a thought, I asked, "Tell me about the kind of person you would admire."

For the next several minutes he described the kind of person he would admire. These are his words (as best I could remember) that I recorded later in my journal: "I would admire someone who was powerful, so long as he was merciful and just. I would admire someone who cared about others, so long as he did not neglect his own children. I would admire someone with integrity, so long as he was not self-righteous. I would admire someone with a cause, so long as he tried to understand the other point of view." (He had participated in some student protests while he was at the university.) "I would admire someone who was willing to give up his life for that cause, so long as he was not simply a martyr for martyrdom's sake." (He had spat upon the grave of an uncle who was a kamikaze. I was not terribly surprised since I had felt similar emotions at the tomb of Thomas à Becket at Canterbury.) "I know this is impossible, but I would settle for someone who was strong, so long as he was loving and kind. You must see my dilemma. Since my mother's death, I cannot find anyone who puts not all of this but any of this together."

My mind was spinning. Suddenly, it was apparent to me that as a highly successful businessman, Tak was near despair with his own inability to put any of this together. At that point I simply opened my Bible and said, "Let me tell you about someone you can admire. What do you know about Jesus Christ?" Although he confessed that he knew practically nothing, he seemed interested, the door was open. Then, trying to remember the characteristics he had just described, I began the story.

For the next hour we talked about Jesus Christ as the Son of a living God who had created us in God's own image but who grieved over our inability to become the people we were created to be. It was a relatively simple task to demonstrate from the Bible that God had intended us to be the kind of people that Tak would admire. It was also relatively simple to describe our own failure. It was then important to speak about God as one who loves us enough not only to reveal the model but to empower us to measure up. Bible verses characterizing Jesus and his provision for our sins seemed to fly off the pages:

Jesus was powerful, yet merciful and just (Matt. 9:18-26).

Jesus cared about others, yet refused to neglect children (Matt. 19:13-15).

Jesus had integrity, yet was not self-righteous (Mark 10:34-45).

Jesus had a cause, yet understood the viewpoints of others (Luke 10:25-37).

Jesus was willing to die for that cause, yet was no martyr for martyrdom's sake (John 10:14-18).

Jesus was strong, yet loving and kind (John 13:31-34).

I was amazed at how the gospel was presented simply by taking Tak's own ideal characteristics and attributing them to Jesus. The last text, which introduces the farewell address of Jesus to his disciples on the eve of the Crucifixion, provided the opportunity to talk about the power of the Holy Spirit to measure up, and the subsequent need for community in order to survive. We talked about that at length. By his own admission, Tak was interested.

As the plane approached our destination, I made my new friend an offer. I would pray for him every day (especially as he anticipated the time with his father and stepmother) until my prayers for reconciliation had been answered. I then promised to continue to pray until he "let me off the hook," until he contacted me and told me that the prayers had been answered, that I was free from my obligation, or that I could pray for something else. He was visibly moved, almost embarrassed. I then added, "Tak, you're not worth fifteen dollars, you're worth at least two hundred and fifty dollars." He was surprised, "You saw me buy the painting? I was hoping no one would notice." I took his hand and pointed toward heaven, "I wasn't the only one who noticed."

Just ten days later, I received a fax from Tak. It read, "You won't believe it. I was not only reconciled with my father but with my stepmother as well. I stayed in their home. Thank you for your prayers. By the way, before I let you off the hook, would you consider praying for ... ?"

Since that time Tak has read several of the books that I recommended (including a few of my own), and, with his wife, has joined a church near Oxford. He has still not let me off the hook. I plan to visit with him soon in his home.

A MUSLIM IN LONDON

Now let me tell you a story that can be told more briefly. Some years ago I was working in London and renting a small room just off Edgeware Road. I noticed that most of the shops in the area were apparently owned by Muslims (there are more Muslims than Christians in London). One afternoon, as I was walking back to my "digs," I decided to buy a sandwich from a neighborhood deli. Since there were no tables in the deli, I made my way to a nearby park and sat on one of the benches to enjoy my supper. I was soon joined by a young man dressed in traditional Arab garb. He seemed eager to talk. So we talked.

For some reason the man wanted to tell me his story. I listened carefully (you might make a note that most people are not accustomed to being listened to as though they have something interesting to say). After nearly an hour, the young man began to talk about Islam. At one point I said, "Tell me about the Islamic Law." He was only too eager to do so. For the next half hour he told me about Afghanistan (the country of his birth), where the Islamic Law ruled supreme. Public executions were common. To catch a thief was to cut off a hand. Women (not men) were stoned for adultery. I thought to myself, "You think the Judeo-Christian law is tough, try this one. At least in ancient Israel, one large stone did the deed; in Afghanistan it took two to three hours." Finally, after listening to him describe some of the more intricate points of the law, I had heard enough. I asked (quite innocently), "Do you really want to obey that law?" Without hesitation, he said, "Of course, I've been trying to obey that law for thirty years." Without so much as a thought, I said, "Let me tell you a story."

We then began to talk about the gospel of Jesus Christ where God provides not only the "law" but the power to fulfill it. He was interested. The door was open. It was apparent that he, like so many others, had become frustrated with his inability to measure up.

It helped that in Islam the archetype Muslim is Abraham. We talked about covenant. He asked wonderful questions:

"If Jesus is so important, then how was Abraham saved when Jesus had not yet been born?"

We talked about faith. For Abraham it was faith in the promise to come. For us it is faith in the promise fulfilled. The cross of Jesus Christ stands in the center of salvation history.

"You're telling me that the only way for me to be faithful to the Islamic Law is to become a Christian. Would I still be a Muslim?"

I explained that he would be a follower of Jesus who could now obey the Islamic Law.

"For me to confess to be a follower of Jesus would alienate me from my own people. Are you absolutely sure it's worth it?"

With all of the sincerity that I could muster, I assured him that it was. We talked about the importance of community. I promised to find him some Muslim Christians who would provide him with the kind of support that would sustain him in his Christian walk.

"How do I know that I can remain faithful to Jesus? Muhammad created a perfect law. I'm not perfect. I don't pray as I should. I have cheated my friends. I have lied to my family so that they no longer trust me. I have failed miserably. Jesus, according to you, was a 'perfect' man. I'm still not perfect. I'm sick of failure."

We talked at length about the need to repent and to accept the forgiveness of God. We talked about reconciliation with God, ourselves, and those around us. We then talked about the power of the Holy Spirit available through faith in Jesus Christ. I promised him that if he was willing to risk faith in Jesus Christ as Savior and Lord, the Holy Spirit would empower him to overcome his failure, would bear witness with his spirit that he was a child of God, and would confirm the truth of his newfound faith in Jesus Christ. He would know in his heart what he was confessing with his mouth. It would not all be easy, but God would be just as faithful to him as to Abraham.

He seemed skeptical. I then asked, "What would keep you from putting this to the test, right now?" He rolled his eyes, but smiled, "My family." I said, "Let me make a suggestion. Go and talk to those members of your family who love you the most. Describe your frustration over your inability to be faithful to the Islamic Law. Admit that you have disappointed them. Ask for their forgiveness. Then tell them about the power of the Holy Spirit available through faith in Jesus Christ that would enable you to change, and about your desire to put this faith to the test. In the meantime, I will pray that they understand, and, if you're willing, we can meet here same time tomorrow." There were tears in his eyes. He simply thanked me and left.

I don't know when I've prayed so hard. The next day I arrived early to pray some more, but he was already there. His family had been grateful for his repentance, but they were uncertain about his becoming a Muslim Christian. I'll never forget his words, "If you can promise me one more time that it is worth it, I'm willing to risk it." We prayed together. Over the next five weeks we met together regularly. We found a group of Muslim Christians in a church pastored by a man who I knew would disciple him. We corresponded for years before I lost contact. I still pray for him on occasion. He taught me a great deal and I thank God for his friendship.

THE ARCHITECT

Some years ago I wrote of an encounter with a young man on a plane bound from San Francisco to New Zealand. There I told only the beginning of the story. My father and I were settling into our seats when a young man sat down next to me. He was a landscape architect who worked for a large West Coast firm. After some small talk, he asked me what I did for a living.

"I'm a minister," I replied.

He responded immediately that he was an atheist.

Somewhat intrigued, I asked, "How does a man who gets to work with nature's beauty as a landscape architect get to be an atheist?"

He chuckled, "Just lucky, I guess."

At that point my father nudged me and whispered, "Son, this man is going to be tough."

Perhaps feeling a bit apologetic, the man then asked, "So, why would anyone want to be a minister?"

I turned to him and said, "Let me ask you another question. If you could know for certain that there really is a God who loves and cares for you and who makes a power available to sustain you in your life, would you be interested?"

With apparent conviction, he said, "You bet."

Looking at him rather intently, I simply added, "That's why I'm a minister. I want to help people just like you come to know that there really is a God who loves and cares for you and who makes a power available to sustain you in your life."

Somewhat to my surprise—God help my unbelief—he said, "Tell me more." Since he had not far to run and we were on a long transcontinental flight, that is exactly what I did. The turnaround from one who was resistant and proud in his atheism to one who encouraged me to talk about God took less than sixty seconds. Now, rather than working against me, the man actually asked me to talk about the source of this God-given power.

So, what was the hook? As you might imagine, my architect friend envisioned himself as a "free-thinker," a bit of a maverick with an IQ matched only by his RQ (rebellion quotient). Yet, he was caught by the phrase, "a God who loves and cares and makes a power available to sustain you in your life." Although young, athletic, and financially secure, he sensed a need for help; but God and religion had long been discarded as an old legalism that drove its adherents into fits of temporary submission (not unlike John Wesley's "transient fits of repentance").

His attempts to compensate involved several of the popular "self-help" philosophies, which he soon found equally frustrating. He wanted this power. The door was open.

We continued to talk and, somewhat to my surprise, this man was not as self-assured as I had imagined—they never are. His business was doing well, but he wanted more. He wanted something to sustain him in his quest for meaning and he had despaired in the pursuit. That was the beginning of the story. Now for the rest.

I remember thinking to myself, "This is just too easy." Then the real issue surfaced. He was gay, and from what I could tell, that was the reason he was miserable. Let me give you an abbreviated account of the conversation that ensued.

Like my Muslim friend above, he asked wonderful questions:

"Does God love me as a homosexual? I've been gay as long as I can remember. Didn't God make me this way? Must I change to be a Christian? God knows I've tried to change. In fact, I no longer sleep around; I have a relationship with only one man. Isn't that the point, not to be promiscuous? And if that is the point, then why am I still miserable?"

I felt my father stir in the seat next to me. I glanced at him and noticed that his eyes were closed; he was no doubt praying.

I then turned to my seatmate and began to explain as best I could. First, I assured him that it was no more of a sin to be same-sex oriented than to be blind, and that God loved him just the way he was. He seemed to relax a bit. I then explained that the sin is in yielding to the temptation of sex outside the context of marriage. Since the Bible makes no provision for homosexual marriage and clearly condemns the homosexual act itself, we first of all talked about the power to overcome the temptation, and then we talked about a God who can heal the "mechanism gone wrong," just as Jesus healed the man born blind. Thinking that I might have lost him here, I was relieved to find him still interested.

We then talked about the issue of promiscuity, whether homosexual or heterosexual. He admitted that this was wrong. I added, "I believe that sexual orientation (in all but a very few cases) is learned, conditioned. We tend to act out what we think we are. If you think you are gay, you act gay. If you think you are straight, you act straight. Most gays are recruited by older gays and are led to believe a lie. I know plenty of people who only think that they are gay, and are living out that lie." I was losing him.

"Wait, let me finish." I liked this man and sensed the Holy Spirit at work. If I could keep him on board, I knew that I could help him. So I pressed on. "Regardless of what you feel, God does not create homosexuals; God creates people with all sorts of problems. Although you do not have to be heterosexual to be Christian, I believe you must be celibate outside the context of marriage to be at peace with yourself. Even though you may not believe that God exists, I believe that God is at work within you. That's why you are miserable. That also means there is hope. God, if there is a God, can restore you to what you were meant to be. There is something in you that knows that this is true, and will not let you rest until you are whole." Wonderfully, he was still with me.

We then talked at length about the power of the Holy Spirit available through faith in Jesus Christ. If he was willing to place his faith and trust in Christ, the Holy Spirit not only would convict but could empower him to overcome, so that he could be at peace with himself.

To make a very long story short, we continued to talk for the next six hours. We became good friends. I promised him that even if he did not become a Christian, neither God nor I would love him any less.

Our paths crossed many times after that first encounter. Although he was still actively gay, each time we met I would assure him of my continued love and support. Then one day, while we were driving on a California freeway, I asked him one more time, "Are you ready to accept Jesus Christ?" He later described his response, "For some reason I was ready, and I heard myself say, 'Yes.'"

Since that time my friend has not only been celibate, but has peace with God and himself and has begun a ministry to homosexuals called "BeWhole." He grieves that his former lover has died from AIDS. He knows that God not only saved him from misery, but saved his life as well. My friend is now in a community of believers that not only disciple him but also provide support for his ministry.

THE TRAIN TO VLADIVOSTOK

"Hello, boys, my name is Alex. I'm from Vladivostok." I did not feel like a boy after two weeks of wandering around China. Those were words from a man who was walking past us on the platform of a train station in Chang Chung, a city in northern Manchuria. As we boarded the train, this man and his companions took the cabin next to ours. As the train left the station, headed for Vladivostok, Alex invited us in for a visit. What a visit!

Within minutes, I and three of my students found ourselves chatting with three Soviet and two Chinese communists. Those were heady days (the fall of 1990, just before the collapse of the U.S.S.R.), and our conversation reflected it. Almost immediately, as the vodka and pickled quail eggs were passed around (we respectfully declined the vodka but ate enough of the eggs to make up for it), Alex began to complain about his growing frustration with communism. He insisted that it made far too many demands and offered very little incentive. One of the Soviets, a leader in the Communist Party, challenged him, and the debate was on. My students and I watched as they engaged in what we hoped (though we were not always sure) was a friendly exchange.

Several hours later, an interesting thing happened. By that time they knew that we were Christians. Alex began to question us about our beliefs, and then admitted that when he was a small child his mother had taken him to a local priest for baptism. With apparent reluctance, the other men also confessed that although they were "officially" atheists, they too had been baptized as children. Suddenly Alex, undaunted by his associates, was asking questions:

"Has God given up on me because I am a communist? What is a Christian? Am I a Christian simply because I was baptized as a child?"

Immediately, it was obvious to me that although none of these men had followed up on their baptism, there was a residual curiosity in them about God, especially in Alex. Although his friends were resistant and teased him for asking such questions, Alex was open.

I talked about how the Communist Party set an example for Christian community. Christians who were as committed to their fellow Christians as communists were to their comrades enjoyed a fellowship that was blessed by God and empowered by the Holy Spirit. God did not give up on people because of a certain ideology. Alex could be a communist and still be a Christian if he was willing, in spite of the Party's denial of God, to place his faith and trust in Jesus Christ, whose Spirit would then authenticate the existence of God.

We then talked some about Karl Marx and socialism, in contrast with an atheistic communism. Jesus himself was probably a socialist in the sense that he was committed to feeding the hungry, clothing the naked, and visiting the sick and imprisoned. Jesus talked more about money than he did about prayer. Too much money bred corruption. Giving to the poor out of love and concern for others was absolutely indispensable to Christian principle.

Although his companions were dozing, perhaps from too much vodka, Alex was still interested. I explained our belief that although becoming a Christian is more than being baptized as an infant (God bless his mother), the Holy Spirit works through baptism to draw us to faith in God. I then suggested that the Spirit of God had prepared him for a moment such as this when he would be asked to repent of his sins and believe in Jesus Christ as God's provision for his salvation.

For some reason, none of us were surprised when Alex smiled and said, "I'm ready. Pray for me, so that I can become a Christian."

I wish that this story had a happy ending. After we prayed with Alex, he seemed relieved. His parting words were that his mother would be proud. As we left to return to our own cabin, we promised to meet with him the following morning. We were excited.

Sometime during the middle of the night we heard a horrible scream, a crash, and then total silence. Since the commotion obviously had come from the cabin of Alex and his companions, we were tempted to ask if everything was all right, but decided against it. The next morning we could not wait to speak with our new convert. When we knocked on the cabin door, his companions merely said that Alex was missing. Since we were then arriving at our destination at Yangi, while the train was traveling on to Vladivostok, there was no opportunity for further inquiry. We will probably never know what really happened. We were bewildered. Was Alex murdered by his companions and then thrown out the window of the moving train? That would be difficult to accept. One thing I know for certain. That night Alex became a Christian and his mother (God rest her soul) was proud.

A CONCERT IN BRAZIL

I have a friend who is a Brazilian evangelist. He is also an incredible musician. He took me and several of my students to Brazil for a series of preaching missions. Since his reputation as a musician was well known throughout Brazil, he would simply announce a concert in one of the local auditoriums and people would gather. He played to packed houses, night after night. The band would begin and he would sing for thirty minutes to an hour. He would then ask one of us to preach for ten minutes, no more, while he interpreted. Finally, he would give an invitation. Those responding would line up in four lines. One line was for conversion. Another was for the baptism of the Holy Spirit (although it is not my theology to separate conversion and

Spirit baptism, I did not go there to argue theology but to do ministry, so I went along happily). The next line was for healing (physical, emotional, and spiritual). The last line was for deliverance.

Since my students and I could not speak Portuguese, we prayed with these people in English, even though they could not understand what we were praying. The Holy Spirit communicated in spite of the language barrier. I was amazed at the results. Significant ministry took place in every line.

The music, more than the preaching, communicated the gospel. The invitation introduced a time of ministry, which frequently went on for several hours. My students and I (as we were instructed) "prayed the gospel" as we laid our hands on our Brazilian friends. Let me share just one of the many stories.

Deana, one of the students, had spent most of the evening holding one of the many children who had been brought forward for prayer. Eventually, the child's mother came for prayer as well. Somewhat to Deana's surprise, the mother spoke some English. She had been watching and listening. Deana, still holding the child, asked the mother how she should pray. Placing a hand on the head of her child, the mother said, "Pray for my baby, and for me. We would like to know Jesus." The request was simple, straightforward. It was her heart's desire. I have frequently said that one's heart's desire becomes a perpetual prayer. We pray that which is most important, almost without thinking. Furthermore, if one's heart's desire is consistent with the mind of Jesus, that prayer guarantees an anointing. Deana helped the woman to pray, and since the desire to know Jesus is obviously consistent with the mind of Jesus, the anointing came. The woman is not only being discipled in a community of believers but now has a significant ministry of her own among the poor of Rio.

PREACHING IN AFRICA

It might be helpful to illustrate the principles of a transcultural gospel as preached in a sermon. Two years ago, while in Africa, I had several opportunities to put this to the test. Let me describe just one of the experiences.

Several students and I flew to Africa for a two-and-a-half-week mission in Kenya and Uganda. A former student who was from Uganda had prepared an extensive itinerary. We quickly found ourselves on the "AIDS highway" in a small Kenyan town near the Ugandan border. My students were divided up into teams and sent into the bush for ministry in villages where many of the Africans had never seen a white person. While they were surrounded by grass huts, I was left behind to teach in a local church and then to preach in the open air from a platform in the town center. As a gas generator powered the large speakers, people gathered, some from shopping in the local market, some waiting for buses, some pausing on bicycles, and some simply milling around, watching curiously as some of the women danced to the music being sung by a team of African Christians. Drums were beating as if to summon the crowd. Silence fell as I began to preach.

The text was from Mark 2, the healing of the paralytic. As an African pastor stood to translate into Swahili, I suddenly imagined a story. I began to describe the life of a twelve-year-old African boy named Jerugo, the son of a village shaman, a witch doctor. Jerugo was headstrong—determined to go his own way. One day, just before Jerugo became a man, an argument exploded between him and his father. The father, shamed by Jerugo's disrespect, made a vow. He would refuse to eat until his son had repented. Three weeks into his fast, the father died. Jerugo was filled with guilt. He had murdered his father.

Many years later Jerugo, now a man, became wealthy. He had a wife and many children. He had fields of maize and cotton, potatoes and rice. His banana trees flourished. His goats and chickens multiplied. Still, he carried the guilt of his father's death. He could never measure up. In an attempt to prove himself, he became more and more reckless. One day, as he was hunting alone, he was mauled by a lion so that he was paralyzed and could not walk. He thought to himself, "Finally, I am being punished for my sin. I am about to die." Inexplicably, the lion suddenly stopped the attack, stood, and stared. Jerugo begged the lion to finish the job, but the lion ran away, leaving him only paralyzed. Jerugo decided that since he had not died, he must be miserable for the rest of his life. He crawled into the bush and hid in a cave to escape the taunts of the village shamans who would associate his paralysis with the sin against his father. He avoided these religious leaders not because he believed they were wrong, but because he knew they were right. Guilt-ridden and alone except for a few faithful friends, Jerugo had no one who could comfort him.

Then one day four of Jerugo's friends came to him with the news of a great shaman who was visiting the villages and healing the sick. This shaman, unlike the other shamans, spoke with an authority from on high, far beyond superstition and myth. He had power over demons. He made the blind to see, the deaf to hear, and the lame to walk—his name was Jesus. These friends knew that if they could just get their unfortunate companion into the presence of Jesus, Jesus would heal him. After much persuasion, Jerugo allowed his friends to take him to this great shaman who was teaching in a neighboring village. As they approached the village, their hearts fell. The huge crowd in the large hut where Jesus was teaching made it impossible to get anywhere near him. Then they had an idea. By placing ladders against the roof, they carried Jerugo up to the top and slowly began to remove the thatch over the spot where Jesus was teaching. They then lowered Jerugo and his pallet on ropes through the hole in the roof and into the room in front of Jesus, throwing the ropes in after him, dusting off their hands, and saying to themselves, "Job well done. Now it is up to Jesus."

At that point, Jesus says an interesting thing: "Your sins are forgiven." Immediately, Jerugo has a vision of his father in the room there with him. They are in each other's arms, hugging and kissing, tears of forgiveness streaming down their cheeks. After so many years, Jerugo and his father are reconciled.

The shamans, however, are standing along the side of the hut objecting among themselves: "Who does this man think he is? Only God can forgive sins."

Jesus, knowing their thoughts, speaks to these shamans, "You say this man is unable to walk because of his sin." They nodded. "You have a saying among your teachers that no one can be healed without the forgiveness of sins." Again, they nodded. "You say I have no authority to forgive sins and therefore this man cannot be healed by me." Once again, they nodded, this time more vigorously. Jesus then says, "OK, watch this." Looking at Jerugo, he says with an authority filled with compassion and understanding, "Pick up your bed and walk." Since Jerugo had already received what he needed most, he had picked up his pallet and had begun to walk before he realized that his body had been healed as well. As he leaves the hut he starts to walk faster and faster, then to trot, then to run. He runs all the way to his village, where he sees his wife teaching several of their children. Although her back is to him, the children see him coming and their eyes are as big as jack fruit. They have not seen their father walk, much less run, for years. As he approaches, his wife turns and he says only two words, *"I'm forgiven."* Jerugo explains how he was forgiven by Jesus and then healed as well. He and his whole family then place their faith and trust in Jesus Christ and find peace with the living God.

The story of Jerugo has been taken from a similar story told in the Bible. It is significant that in both stories the friends of the paralytic know that if they can get their friend into the presence of Jesus that Jesus will heal him. Jesus says, "For where two or three come together in my name, there am I with them" (Matt. 18:20). Since far more than that are gathered here in his name, we can be assured of his presence. I, like the four friends, am convinced that if you will submit your diseases to him (whether they be of body, mind, or spirit), Jesus will heal you. Submit to him now by coming forward and receiving the prayers of those here who would like to pray with you in his name.

Out of a crowd of nearly five hundred, many came forward to receive the forgiveness of sins and a healing touch from the body of Jesus Christ who lives on in the church. A gathering of local believers prayed and then took those being saved aside for more personal instruction and follow-up.

THE GUIDE IN HAVANA

Last year I was in Cuba. One of our young communist guides took us to a square in old Havana. As we were standing before a rather imposing statue, I asked, "Who is that?"

With obvious pride the guide said, "That is one of our greatest patriots, Carlos Manuel de Céspedes."

I asked, "What did he do?"

He said, "He was the first to free his slaves in 1865 and the first to organize a resistance movement against the Spanish oppressors."

I was impressed, "That is wonderful."

The guide said, "Yes, but there is more. The Spaniards captured his son and threatened to kill him if Céspedes did not back down from the resistance. When he refused, they murdered his son."

I winced, "That's horrible."

His enthusiasm seemed to build, "Yes, but there's more. Our fore-fathers so identified with his example that the relationship between this great patriot and the Cuban people led to our independence and Cuba became a republic in 1902."

I had an insight (some would say a bit of a "no brainer"), "There is an interesting precedent for all of that. God established a covenant with a people and when they were enslaved in Egypt, God (like your well-known patriot) freed them from an oppressor."

The guide said, "That is wonderful."

I said, "Yes, but there is more. God also chose to free the people from the power of sin and offer forgiveness of sins to those who place their faith in his son Jesus Christ."

The guide said, "Yes, I've heard. Is that important?"

I said, "Yes, but there is more. Our freedom cost God the life of his only Son as an atonement for those sins."

The guide said, "That's too bad."

I said, "Yes, but there is more. God raised his Son from the dead and has sent us his Spirit that we might be victorious over sin and death."

The guide asked: "How does that work?"

I said, "Just as your forefathers identified with the example of Car-los Manuel de Céspedes that you might be free from the Spanish oppressors, God asks that we identify with him by placing our faith and trust in his son Jesus Christ. Would you be willing to trust God, as your forefathers trusted Carlos Manuel de Céspedes, that you might be freed from the power of sin and death?"

He said, "I think I would."

He attended the worship service that evening, and the local

church along with subsequent missionary teams are providing the follow-up.

Let me close this chapter with an interesting insight from my neighborhood friend from the dinner party. During our last visit he was open, nearly bold, in his willingness to talk about those who had influenced him most for God. Then, one afternoon a few weeks after this talk, we chatted as he was burning some brush. He was curious about exactly what he needed to do to become a Christian. Although we had gone over this before, I attempted to explain once again. If he was willing for God to take from him those things not yet yielded to God, those areas of resistance that he believed to be unpleasing to God (repentance), and with his willingness to trust Jesus Christ to forgive and empower him to overcome those things that would attempt to swallow him (faith), "low pressure" could be created. The Holy Spirit would then move to that low pressure and help him establish a personal relationship with the God who loved and cared for him. His response somewhat surprised me. "Why would God be so hot to have a relationship with a man like me?" I thought we had covered that ground before as well. Once again, I explained that God saw him as he himself saw his own children and that God loved him like he loved his own children. Then my neighbor remembered. "We've been over this before, haven't we?" I nodded. Then he said, "I just need to hear it one more time, just to make certain the rules haven't changed. I get a bit confused with some of the things I have been reading that make the whole process sound a lot more difficult. Let me think about it." Believe it or not, I changed the subject and we began to talk about something else.

CHAPTER EIGHT

Putting It All to Work—for You

Since it would appear that the concepts described here work in my sphere of influence, let's see if they can work in yours.

When we are looking for assistance in an evangelistic endeavor, it can be helpful to read about the successes and/or failures of others; but if we do not see the relevance for our own situation, or if we are not properly motivated, or if we cannot teach the principles so they can be assimilated by others, then not much has been accomplished.

RELEVANCE FOR YOU

In order to test these concepts I took my case to others to see if these tools would assist them in their own evangelistic endeavors. My first confirmation came as I began to teach these principles to students and friends. Not only did they know of similar experiences, but *their own testimonies* bore this out as well.

I recently received this letter from one of my students:

As a little girl I equated God with my father, who expected perfect performances from me and was never satisfied. As a result, I believed

God to be like Santa, watching to see if I'm good or bad and dispensing his love based on my performance.

Only after I accepted Christ and began to mature in faith did I begin to question my image of God and begin to discover that he might be a better Father for me than was my earthly father. Yet, even into my early married years, I was bound by a need to perform for God and others, to hide any faults and never be wrong. Then, my Walk to Emmaus experience [a weekend spiritual retreat emphasizing God's grace and community] brought me face-to-face with the fact that I really wanted and needed God to be in control of my life, and part of giving over that control involved being "real" with God and allowing him to work in areas where I was less than perfect. I fell in love with God; I was nearly overwhelmed by his unconditional love.

Gradually, since that time, I have found great joy, but always knowing that I could never love God as much as he loves me. Then, as my call to ordained ministry began to be revealed, I hit a wall. I could not speak the word of God from the pulpit, or consecrate and serve communion to people—that was too much of an honor and privilege. God then showed me that that Word and Sacrament was exactly what I was being called to and he had already made me worthy enough. Ironically, by turning away from the need to perform in order to be more worthy or acceptable to God, I have opened myself to what I sought. God does all things for me. I can't do it; but he can. Thus, I live now in the joy of knowing that as I study, pray, and do ministry, it is not by my efforts, but by his Spirit and Grace. What is important in my life is to become better equipped to serve my Lord and Savior as I am minister, pastor, friend, or counselor. My satisfaction comes from giving back to God some little bit of the joy he gives to me. I am finding myself able to see people with his eyes and to love people I never found lovable. He is rooting out of me condemnation and judgment and replacing it with exhortation and love. It occurs to me that maybe God is calling me to build bridges between those of other races or theologies or lifestyles and be a reconciler. What a privilege that would be![1]

Those of you familiar with the Walk to Emmaus weekend know that the appeal there is to experience God as a God of grace who

1. This is the personal testimony of Mary Powell.

accepts us where we are and who empowers us to serve others not out of our own strength but in God's strength (see Phil. 4:13).

A friend writes:

> I embraced Christ chiefly because the conditional love of the world, and the conditional love I had for myself, had finally crushed my spirit. My identity had been destroyed one too many times, again having fallen to pieces after another season of dancing precariously upon the border between approval and disapproval.
>
> I threw up my arms. I could not make my brother accept me. I could not make the girlfriends love me. I could not make the companies hire me; or make the ones that did hire me embrace every little thing that I did and view me as a visionary who could carry them toward greatness. I could not vicariously make my football team become the champions for all time. I could not make life fall into neat, thirty-minute sitcom packages of resolved endings. I could not make all my moments ones of romantic, powerful memories that would lay the foundation for greater and greater shining benchmarks, when the world and all who knew me would admire my poise upon the apex of my pedestal ... when those who had rejected me would long for my presence.
>
> My journey with the Lord is a long, slow embrace that continues to tighten. In its inception, it was analogous to a pair of high school freshmen awkwardly slow-dancing at their first homecoming ball, not daring to get too close. It has been progressing into a more comfortable two-step as the relationship deepens, moving toward the smooth, timeless, and effortless waltz of two golden anniversary souls who have known each other inside and out.
>
> The old tapes continue to play—but do not dominate the ballroom soundtrack as they once did. The old man remains alive on the dance floor, seeking to cut in, but he has competition.
>
> The reliance upon the lure of the world is still my deepest instinct, but the blow of the pain that follows yet another disillusionment is healed by the touch of the Jesus who will not let the dance come to an end. He urges me to move a little closer with each note that is played. Rather than seeking to be the homecoming king, he urges me to let the King come home and live in my heart.[2]

2. This is the personal testimony of John M. De Marco.

John Wesley sometimes referred to his own need to measure up as the old grasshopper. The grasshopper lives on but will yield to the one who is greater (see 1 John 4:4)—competition indeed!

Another student writes:

> I was brought up in an upper-middle-class home. My parents (highly educated) both worked so we could enjoy a lifestyle not available to them when they were children. Although my parents were loving, there was no emphasis on God. We were "Christians" because we were Americans. Since I am reasonably intelligent and like to think for myself, at age twelve I started to question some of their values. My father reacted and we began to argue. His philosophy seemed to be that all of life is appearances: look good and all is well. It is not what you know, but who you know. Success is measured in dollars, not sense. Work hard. Work hard. Work hard. Then, I began to react. At age fifteen, realizing that I was never going to measure up to my father's expectations, and close to despair, I began smoking pot.
>
> A year later the drinking began. After months of arguments with my parents, a DUI, and alcoholic binges that nearly killed me, I began doing LSD instead. I lived totally for myself. Frustrated and looking for change, I even bought a motorcycle, but still had bouts with deep depression.
>
> Finally, I realized that my life was totally out of control. If I wanted to live, I needed to change, but I did not know how. My Christian acquaintances had not greatly impressed me. One night, in total frustration, I decided to try God, just in case. I prayed, "God, if you are there you've got to help me." That may not sound like much, but don't knock it. God called that prayer "faith," and when I awoke the next morning, I felt different. I felt I had been changed. Some months later someone said something to me about Jesus and instantly I knew that I had received a personal visitation from him that night that had enabled me to overcome a way of life that was about to consume me. The next day I went to a local Christian bookstore and bought a Bible and have been on fire ever since. Praise God![3]

Once again, repentance and faith in Jesus is the key that turns the lock that opens the door from the law of sin and death to the law of the Spirit of life (see Rom. 8:1-2).

3. This is the personal testimony of Todd Taum.

Not only did my students and friends acknowledge these principles at work in their own lives, they were eager to test the concepts as they shared the gospel themselves in cross-cultural settings. Here are a few of those testimonies, at home and abroad.

One of my students went into a mall (a tough assignment) to test our principles. The verbatim went something like this:

> I approached a man who was sitting on a bench. He looked bored, but I was too nervous to initiate the conversation. As I sat down, he nodded and said, "Hello."
>
> Feeling more confident, I decided to come out with it. "I'm a seminary student with an assignment. In order to pass one of my courses, I must ask three people to listen to a brief presentation of my understanding of the gospel and then ask for a critique as to whether or not it makes any sense. Would you be willing to listen?"
>
> My bench companion simply smiled and said, "Fire away."
>
> I then began to share the principles taught in class, beginning with a question. "If you could ask God to give you just one thing, what would that be?"
>
> Somewhat to my surprise he answered immediately, "Well, I'm not sure just how much I believe in God, but if there is a God, I would ask him to give me strength to be a good husband and father. I've not done that very well. I work too hard and my time seems to be consumed with my small business. I'm sitting here now because I'm just too tired to walk all over this mall with my wife as she shops for our kids."
>
> Nodding my head, I said, "That's a worthy request. I believe God can give you that strength. It seems to me that the key to receiving from God is repentance and faith. Repentance, according to one of my professors, is a willingness for God to take from you the things that keep you from being who it is that God wants you to be. All of us get frustrated trying to do things on our own, especially when our good intentions fall short of expectations. As far as you know your own heart, would you be willing for God to take from you those things that keep you from being a good husband and father?"
>
> He shrugged, "What have I got to lose?"
>
> This was too easy. "You could lose your inability to measure up. Let's talk about faith. As a Christian I believe that God has given us access

to the power of the Holy Spirit that enables us to be not only good husbands and fathers but fulfilled in all areas of our lives. God promises that if we will dare to repent of our sins and believe in the saving power of his Son, Jesus Christ, he will grant us abundant life."

"That's easier said than done. I used to ask God for the things that preachers on TV said I could have if I would only believe. I asked God to heal my brother from cancer and he died, begging to die. I lost faith when I realized that God really is not able to make a difference. All those promises in the Bible are wishful thinking. Daring to believe is tougher than you think."

"Please don't think I'm making light of your frustration, but maybe it's not really so tough. It seems to me that many of us try to make it more difficult than it is. The key lies in your sincere desire to be in right relationship with God, who wants to give you all good things. That sincere desire could lead you to commit all that you know of yourself to all that you know of God by asking his Son, Jesus, to come and live in your heart."

He smiled, "Young man, I know you mean well, but that does not make a lot of sense. I've worked six, seven days a week for seven and a half years in my business in order to get ahead and provide for my family. Nothing comes that easily. I understand something of what you say, but most of it is too good to be true."

He was getting restless, so I blurted out, "Try it, you'll like it! You pray this prayer and I know in my heart that God will answer you. 'Please God, take my inability and replace it with your ability as I try my best to put my faith and trust in your Son, Jesus Christ.' To use your own words, you have nothing to lose. Doesn't it make sense to try? Here's my number. Call me if you like and let me know if this doesn't work. If it does I can help you find a bunch of folks who would be willing to help you in your newfound faith." I handed him my number on a slip of paper. He took it, looked at it, and said, "I'll think about it." I thanked him sincerely for his attention and walked away.[4]

I wish I could give you the rest of the story, but it is still to be seen. I gave this student high marks for the case. I believe the principles were clearly at work.

4. This is the personal testimony of someone who wishes to remain anyonymous.

Here is another testimony from a student whose sharing of the gospel demonstrates the concepts in still another way. This took place over the entire semester.

Rod Morris had been a professional football player with the San Francisco 49ers before he blew out his knee. Now, fully rehabilitated, he made his living fighting fires as part of the Youngstown, Ohio, fire department. He was a man of men in everyone's eyes but his own. Life had become a series of failed reaches, one after another. Most who knew him admired his manly stature and confident demeanor, but Rod saw himself as a failure. Each venture in life was a disappointing attempt to prove to himself his own manliness. His broken marriage and part-time dad status were constant reminders of his nonsuccess in being a man worthy of respect.

Rod began attending church with Linda, a pleasant and attractive woman he had been dating for a short time. They shared much in common. Both were divorcees; both had two teenage children; and both wanted to make a success of their lives this time around. For Rod, that meant finding acceptance of himself as a real man, although he wasn't sure just what that was. He knew it was something that he wasn't.

Week after week Rod would sit in church attentively, but he was never a part of the worship. He stood or sat motionless as the congregation sang. Exiting the assembly, he always gave me a strong and friendly handshake, but words were few.

At Linda's suggestion, and to the surprise of many, Rod signed up for the weekend trip to Detroit for the second annual Promise Keepers rally. He joined sixty-three other men from the church, retaining a polite but cautious disposition. This was a new adventure. Buses were loaded with men engaged in spirited conversation and laughter without the off-color stories and boisterous attempts to prove themselves to the others. How different from the bus and plane rides he had known as a football player. He had no way of knowing the significance of the next forty-eight hours.

The Friday-night service began with an immediate burst of energy. The stadium filled with men. At the request of the leader on stage all rose to their feet in a unified acclamation of the Lordship of Jesus. Some shouted, some whistled, some clapped, and some even cried. Rod just stood there at a loss for words. Silent and suspicious, he observed the face of the speaker and the endless mass of smiling men. Was this for real, or like the all-too-familiar pre-game hype? At the close of the service more than five thousand men left their seats, making their way to the platform. While others watched and prayed from their seats, these men went down on the gridiron, kneeling, praying, and crying, many of them yielding their beings to Christ. Rod just watched and wondered.

The next morning began with a spirited session of praise in song. For the first time, Rod was singing! The worship leader, noticing the mixed assembly of colors and cultures, challenged the men to a time of reconciliation and acceptance of one another. Immediately, white men were embracing black men with tears and words of apology for their personal prejudices and for the offenses of a nation's history toward all people of color. Suddenly, Rod was weeping! Visibly, this giant of a man was shrinking in submission to the work of the Holy Spirit. Soon, he would be able to identify with all that was happening, in the name of Jesus!

In the afternoon and evening sessions, Rod sang with all his heart! He was no longer observing, scrutinizing, or evaluating. Rod was releasing, praising, and radiating something from within. Rod was enjoying life like he had never known it before. He had not yet put all the pieces together; he was still confused and full of questions; but he knew something big was taking place in his life. The journey home was entirely different. A few of the men shared with him and answered his lingering questions.

The next evening, back at the church with a handful of friends accompanying Linda, I had the privilege of baptizing Rod into Christ. The next Sunday and every Sunday thereafter, if Rod was not on duty, he was at worship, singing, smiling, and standing taller than ever. He later confessed, "All my life I have sought to prove my manhood, not just to others, but to myself. Football didn't do it, my marriage didn't work, and the fire department failed to give me that illusive assurance of being a real man! Nothing worked until now!" He had found Jesus. Rod had tried his whole life, looking in all the wrong places, to find that which was never far from him.

Though Rod and Linda are no longer dating, they both have remained faithful. If you were to go to the Greenford Christian Church this Sunday, chances are you would find a big man with a broad smile and a booming voice in the choir loft, singing praises to the one who freed Rod from himself to become a real man of God. In Christ, he found that elusive dream. In faithfulness, he had gained peace within.[5]

5. This is a personal from Dean Hammond.

R. C. Das, in the book *Evangelical Prophet for Contextual Christianity*, writes, "I became a Christian not because I found Hinduism all weak, or false or bad but because I found its strength, its truth and its goodness not strong, true and good enough as my soul in utter need demanded."[6]

I have always been grateful that the Christian faith is self-authenticating. With our repentance and faith, the Spirit of God bears witness with our spirits that we are children of God (see Rom. 8:16). Once we understand the need, we can be confident that God is faithful. "For no matter how many promises God has made, they are 'Yes' in Christ. And so through him the 'Amen' is spoken by us to the glory of God. Now it is God who makes both us and you stand firm in Christ. He anointed us, set his seal of ownership on us, and put his Spirit in our hearts as a deposit, guaranteeing what is to come" (2 Cor. 1:20-22).

MOTIVATION

One of the most important characteristics of those who seek training is that they are motivated. Never again will I assume that people are motivated to do evangelism. In fact, evangelism in a postmodern world has acquired such a bad rap that it is difficult to find Christians to consider even the best of programs.

A few years ago I moved from Evanston, Illinois, to Wilmore, Kentucky. Just before I left, several students took me to lunch. We sat in a crowded restaurant, and I decided to ask them a question. "What would it take for me to stand on top of this table and say to the people here, 'Friends, I know you have a right to enjoy your meal without my interruption, but I have something I have to say. If you will give me just two minutes to share with you the good news of the power of God available through faith in Jesus Christ, I will never bother you again.' " Already I could see the eyes of several students begin to roll, as if to say, "Please God, do not let him do it." Then one student volunteered. "You would have to believe that everyone here

6. R. C. Das, *Evangelical Prophet for Contextual Christianity*, H. L. Richard, ed. (Delhi: Indian Society for Promoting Christian Knowledge, 1955), pp. 20, 31.

was going to hell." I responded instantly, "Wrong! You could never 'guilt' me into the possibility of making a fool of myself. I refuse to believe that anyone goes to hell because of my disobedience. Where is the justice in that? Only one thing could motivate me to do such a thing—*compassion*. I would have to see everyone here as God sees them, as I see my own children." I think they understood, but were still relieved that this was simply an academic question.

Again, to be filled with the Spirit is to see people as God sees them, as we see our own children. Jesus (and Jeremiah before him) wept over Jerusalem. Seeing people in bondage to sin should break our hearts. I am convinced that one does not have to die to go to hell. Many have lived there long enough. Just this week I found these words on a piece of paper stuffed in some old class notes: "Religion is for those who want to avoid hell. Spirituality is for those who have been there." Hell is all around us; but the One who is in us is greater than the one who is in the world. Last month I saw an automobile bumper with a sticker on either end. One end said, "Stuff happens!" The other end said, "But my God reigns!" Why do I like that?

Jesus was motivated by compassion. Find that word in the New Testament and know that something good is about to happen.

TIPS FOR TRAINING

One of the keys for training is *overcoming resistance*. We have already established that most people are reluctant to do ministry because they fear rejection. There is another problem that is just as debilitating—they assume inadequacy. There is a powerful passage in 1 Corinthians 12:14-26. It insists that "those parts of the body that seem to be weaker are indispensable" (v. 22). I frequently tell my students that our greatest strengths are anointed weaknesses. Anoint pride and it turns to holy boldness. Of course we are inadequate—on our own—but God's grace is sufficient. God has more invested in your ministry than you do. In fact, your life is more important to God than it is to you. Believe it if you can. It could change your life.

Once again, hear a challenge. **Be bold for God.** You put Christianity into principles of supply and demand, and I promise you the demand is out there. This is not to increase your burden—I want only to increase your vision. God could do ministry without us. The point is, God has chosen not to. God has determined either to use us or to return in all of God's glory and claim God's own, if but out of the rubble. Even as you read these words, God's Holy Spirit is at work on every street in every city and hamlet the world over, preparing people for the ministry of the church universal. That is the God's honest truth.

Training not only overcomes resistance, it equips with tools that are flexible enough to work in every sphere of influence. This is not merely "one size fits all." We have not sought some lowest common denominator as if to simplify the gospel. Those books have already been written (including one of my own). What we have done is uncover innate principles that reveal a receptivity to the Word we share. Again, these concepts are not simply cross-cultural in that they communicate from one culture to another; they are transcultural in that they are common to every culture.

One more tip for training is developing trust. How can we share our principles so that others can trust the process enough to risk the challenge? A longtime friend recently popped into my office. He had just returned from England and was telling me about a church in London (Holy Trinity Anglican in Brompton) where the emphasis is on developing trust. It seems that those who visit there sense the fellowship as a haven of rest, a city of refuge. As I pressed for details he explained, "They refuse to judge. Holy Trinity has mastered the art of communicating through pastoral skills. While holding to principles of morality consistent with the New Testament, they are accepting. There is not a whisper of arrogance. That is, they were absolutely secure. They genuinely want to know your story. They want to know what they can do for you and what you can do for the Kingdom."

I found it interesting that as I read their literature they appeared low-key in their Anglican (denominational) connection.[7] An ecumenical spirit embraces the multifaceted aspects of the body of

---

7. You might want to read Nicky Gumbel's *Telling Others: the Alpha Initiative*, Kingsway Publication, 1994, about the work going on at Holy Trinity.

Christ. I was especially taken with the trust that accrues from their refusal to judge others.

As strange as this may sound, last year I tried to take a two-month moratorium on judging others. Let me tell you the story of how this came about. Someone I trust with my life took me to a dinner party. I immediately liked the host and the other guests. They were Episcopalian charismatics, open to the work of the Spirit, with a real appreciation for the sacraments (my kind of people). Then after several hours I began to realize something. Our host was relating to another man at the party with particular affection. After watching them more closely, I learned that he and his special companion had been living together in a homosexual relationship for twenty years. My companion had neglected to warn me about this. This was my dilemma. Although I believe that the homosexual act is sin, I already liked these people. What was I to do? Should I back up and start *un*liking them in order to avoid the implication that I approved of their lifestyle? I did not feel the need. I realized that liking them as *persons*, while rejecting what I believed to be sinful *behavior*, were not incompatible with each other. On the other hand, any impulse to transfer my disapproval of their lifestyle to a disapproval of them personally was a form of judgment. Right then I made a vow. For the next two months I would attempt a moratorium on judging others. For two months I would love people for who they are and let God do the judging. That may seem elementary to you, but I found it impossible. Since judgment comes from feelings of superiority, evidently I feel superior since I found myself breaking my own rule practically every day. I remember asking one of my students, "What would it be like if I simply loved people for who they are and let God do the judging?" Instantly he replied, "Why, that would be like Jesus." Got me! It served me right. I really do not want God's job (I don't care what my wife may have told you). I am called to follow Jesus by accepting and loving people for who they are, and to leave it to God to work out the consequences of those persons' actions and attitudes. After the two-month trial I decided that if trust is to develop in my own attempts to communicate I must extend the moratorium indefinitely. Pray for me.

Surely where training is concerned, nothing can take the place of demonstration. Jesus was the master at show-and-tell. He did ministry so effectively that his disciples said, "Teach us to do that." I not only encourage my students to share, but I frequently take them with me when I go out to preach in local churches. They watch me in conversation without an evangelistic agenda. We have already established that evangelism is God's agenda and when God opens the door we must be ready to walk through it. If someone is hungry, what do you do? You feed them, unless you are a stone. If someone is naked, what do you do? You clothe them, unless you are a brick. If someone is in bondage to the things that would destroy them, what do you do? You tell them about the power of God available through faith in Jesus Christ, unless you just don't care.

But we do care! God has done that to us. God has made us into an incurably caring people who love justice and mercy and want no one to suffer at the hands of the one who has already been defeated. Let God arise.

My next exchange with my neighbor was brief. This time I took the initiative. "Are you ready to repent and place your faith and trust in Jesus Christ?" His immediate response, "No." He was not hostile or resentful, just not ready. Once again, I changed the subject and we talked about something else.

Conclusion

In conclusion, it is important to remember that a transcultural gospel is just that—*a* transcultural gospel. It is not the only way to present the good news of Jesus Christ across cultural boundaries. The principles given here are intended to quicken the mind and stir the spirit. The gospel is not a "Western" gospel. Jesus was hardly bound to one single culture, even his own. In a sense, Jesus cut across all cultures and exposed them to the mind of an eternal God who wants to be known as the one who loves and makes the Holy Spirit available to those who place their trust in the gift of an only Son. So I hope our task has become clear—which **concepts and even ideologies that communicate across cultural boundaries can be used as tools in a gospel presentation that is truly transcultural.**

Furthermore, there are obviously many more transcultural common denominators that can assist the church in the task of an evangelism that is more "user-friendly" across cultural boundaries. The evangelist must always be on the lookout for stories, myths, symbols, rituals, and even pieces of art that can transfer eternal truth from one culture to another. No matter what the setting, God is never left without a witness (see Acts 14:17). I recall a line from a popular movie "God is wooing us with the color purple and is angry when we don't notice." Numerous polls tell us that the whole world is incurably religious. Everyone is looking for meaning and purpose to life.

The problem is that the church's witness is not always that clear. Frequently she vacillates between institutional self-interest and sacrificial giving, between sectarianism and ecumenical fervor, between obscurantism and moments of clarity and purpose, between introvertedness and all-out compassion, between irrelevance and poignancy, ignorance and wisdom, worldliness and godliness, impotence and power—incredible power, power to overcome sin in persons, power to overcome sin in systems, power to demolish strongholds, power to change the world.

The use of transcultural common denominators in the search for a transcultural gospel enables us to hear what people are really saying, or asking. It also teaches us the kinds of things that alienate. I mentioned that two years ago I was in Africa. It did not take long to realize that preaching to tribal peoples without the approval of the tribal council is an offense that defeats the purposes of the gospel. Closer to home, gender references to God make it impossible for some feminists (who might otherwise be open) to hear the gospel from a different perspective. Have you noticed that apart from an occasional quotation I have not made one gender reference to God in the entire book? I hope you were not even aware of it. Trust me, I gave up no theology essential to truth. I simply attempted to practice what I preach.

Communication is hard work. The church has failed all too often because we are simply not speaking the same language, even among ourselves. We do not use words that heal. We grind the proverbial ax in order to say it "our way." Some evangelists fail all too often because they play to stereotypes without a thought to the images they conjure in the minds of the very people they have been called to evangelize. God forgive us. The world has rubbed our noses in charges of torture (during the Inquisition), imperialism (during the Colonial periods), genocide (in Nazi Germany), and even fratricide (in Ireland, Bosnia, and parts of Latin America). Since the world delights in the hypocrisy of Elmer Gantry, Sweet Daddy Grace, and Jim Bakker (who has since repented and seems to be on the way to reestablishing his ministry), this research has attempted to suggest some positive principles that might possibly encourage us. I am weary of only being warned about what *not* to do. There are obviously Christians out there who are doing it well. Wherever there is revival some transcultural needs are being met.

Some of the psychologists are wrong. The most basic needs are not simply sex and aggression; they are love and understanding, perhaps even a search for meaning beyond the limits of a worldly mentality. I have found that few transcultural common denominators plumb the depths of the unseen. There is one exception—an interest (at some point) in things eternal. Something has to make sense of it all. I have frequently thought that if there is no life after death then God is a monster. There is simply too much injustice around this world for this life alone to be all there is. A universal gospel should give us clues to the broader perspective. Let me illustrate.

Some time ago a student came to me for advice. A man in the nursing home where he was serving as a student intern had challenged him with a statement. As the student entered the man's room he could see that both the man's legs had been amputated just above his knees. The man looked at him and said, "God has a good list and God has a hit list and I've been on God's hit list all my life." Instantly, I had an insight: God has no hit list and the world has no good list. The world has only a hit list and God has only a good list. Furthermore, if any of us wait to be happy until we have received what we deserve according this world's expectations, we will never be happy, because "there ain't no justice in this world." The only justice is in God. That's a given as certain as death. In the midst of worldwide injustices the universal mind already suspects this. Consequently, most cultures have little hope according to this world's expectations. A transcultural gospel must, as we have observed, make an appeal for a reality beyond the senses. Little wonder Paul writes, "For what is seen is temporary, but what is unseen is eternal" (2 Cor. 4:18). Put another way, the only things eternal are unseen. The universal mind wants to know.

Since "story" is also transcultural ("Once upon a time . . ." almost always draws attention), let me close with two more. The first is from the Bible.

In 2 Kings 6 the Arameans were at war with Israel. Elisha, by the Spirit, knew where the enemy would strike next and would warn the king of Israel in advance. Eventually, the king of Aram suspected a spy in his own camp—only to be informed that there was a prophet in Israel who knew his thoughts, even his most private ones. The king of Aram demanded, "Bring him to me, now!"

The Aramean army surrounded the little town of Dothan where Elisha lived. Elisha's servant was the first to see the horses and chariots of the mighty army surrounding the town and went to warn Elisha. When Elisha saw the army he said to his servant, "Don't be afraid. Those who are with us are more than those who are with them. O LORD, open his eyes so he may see" (2 Kings 6:16-17). The Lord opened the servant's eyes and what did he see?—chariots of fire on every hill.

Be encouraged. I know the task seems monumental but whether at home or abroad, if we are loving and sensitive toward others, in whatever culture, we can rest assured that the Spirit of God (even now) is preparing the hearts of people the world over to receive the gospel of Jesus Christ. Surely, **those who are with us are more than those who are with them.**

My last story (you might have guessed it) follows up on my friend from the dinner party. Although our last exchange had been brief, once again he was ready to talk about God. I now understood his need to measure up. Again, I wanted him to know about a God who loved and cared and then created, whose power was available to overcome that which sought to consume him. I also knew he needed support. So, we talked about God. We talked at length about his future. What could he do to give his life more meaning and purpose? He was a good man. God would not waste a man with his talents. He was easy to affirm. It was also easy to suggest areas of possible ministry, though he laughed at the word "ministry" and shrugged, "God help me." I also shrugged, "And God doesn't force early retirement."

One day I took him with me to a downtown mission where we served meals to the homeless. He loved it. Soon his creative instincts took over and he suggested other areas of involvement. One day I found him talking with a homeless woman from Pakistan. She was listening carefully. I overheard the name Jesus. Finally, I realized that my friend and I really had communicated about the things of God, and now he was communicating as well.

Now *that* is transcultural!